Birthday Cakes
for Kids

Birthday Cakes
for Kids

Annie Rigg

photography by Sandra Lane

RYLAND
PETERS
& SMALL

LONDON NEW YORK

To my godchildren, Alec,
Izzie, Albie and Tom Tom

Senior designer Megan Smith
Senior editor Céline Hughes
Production manager
   Patricia Harrington
Art director Leslie Harrington
Publishing director Alison Starling

Prop stylist Liz Belton
Indexer Hilary Bird
Diagrams Ray Betts

First published in the
United Kingdom in 2009 by
Ryland Peters & Small
20–21 Jockey's Fields
London WC1R 4BW

www.rylandpeters.com

10 9 8 7 6 5 4 3 2 1

Text © Annie Rigg 2009

Design and photographs
© Ryland Peters & Small 2009

ISBN: 978-1-84597-832-7

A CIP record for this book is available from
the British Library.

Printed and bound in China

• All spoon measurements are level, unless
otherwise specified.
• Ovens should be preheated to the specified
temperature. Recipes in this book were tested
using a regular oven. If using a fan-assisted oven,
follow the manufacturer's instructions for adjusting
temperatures.
• All eggs are medium, unless otherwise specified.
Recipes containing raw or partially cooked egg
should not be served to the very young, very old,
anyone with a compromised immune system or
pregnant women.

contents

the star of the show

One of the most important elements of any child's birthday party has to be the cake. Most people can easily remember their favourite birthday cake from childhood and the excitement in choosing a cake every year. Whether you make the same cake every time or something completely different, a home-made cake simply can't be beaten both for the joy it gives children and the satisfaction of knowing that it's all your work.

I'm lucky to have eager guinea pigs in my small tribe of godchildren, who provided plenty of inspiration for the cakes in this book. I have loved baking since I was a little girl and I hope that they too will soon discover what fun there is to be had in the kitchen sticking, layering, icing and decorating. The results are so rewarding. And who knows, they may even start coming up with some imaginative creations of their own.

Whatever your level of baking skills there's a cake here to suit everyone. There are also a few basic guidelines on pages 10 and 16–19 to help you get the best results whenever you bake.

Most of the cakes in this book can be made ahead of time and can be kept for up to 2 days (un-iced), well wrapped in clingfilm, or frozen un-iced and defrosted the day before the party. Cupcakes keep well in the freezer and defrost quickly, making them an easy and convenient option. In fact, cupcakes are a great starting point if you are nervous about your baking skills.

If you don't want to test your construction skills then choose a cake that can be shaped by cutting around a template rather than one that requires measuring and layering. Most of the cakes here are easy for the novice baker – just remember to allow yourself plenty of time to complete the icing and final decorations. Remember that any imperfections can be cunningly disguised under a layer of icing, sweets and sprinkles.

No matter which cake you choose to make for your child's birthday, you can be sure of smiles of delight when they are presented with a home-baked creation. And if at first you feel unsure about assembling, layering and decorating, there's always the old favourite – chocolate cake. Don't forget the candles!

the basics

basic vanilla sponge

This is the most basic vanilla sponge mixture, which can be adapted to introduce different flavours (see end of recipe). It is used in many of the recipes in this book as it makes a good base for cakes which need to be cut up and re-assembled, and it tends to be liked by most children. I have provided four quantities to suit individual recipes but the method remains the same regardless of the quantity you use. For best results I suggest using an electric free-standing mixer. Before you start baking make sure all the ingredients are at room temperature, the oven is preheated with the oven shelf in the correct position and the relevant cake tins have been prepared. The oven temperatures given throughout the book are for a conventional oven; if you are using a fan oven, adjust the temperature according to the manufacturer's instructions.

EXTRA LARGE

350 g unsalted butter,
   at room temperature
350 g caster sugar
6 large eggs, beaten
2 teaspoons vanilla extract
350 g plain flour
5 teaspoons baking powder
4–5 tablespoons milk,
   at room temperature

LARGE

250 g unsalted butter,
   at room temperature
250 g caster sugar
4 large eggs, beaten
1 teaspoon vanilla extract
250 g plain flour
4 teaspoons baking powder
3–4 tablespoons milk,
   at room temperature

MEDIUM

175 g unsalted butter,
   at room temperature
175 g caster sugar
3 large eggs, beaten
1 teaspoon vanilla extract
175 g plain flour
3 teaspoons baking powder
3 tablespoons milk,
   at room temperature

SMALL

125 g unsalted butter,
   at room temperature
125 g caster sugar
2 large eggs, beaten
½ teaspoon vanilla extract
125 g plain flour
2 teaspoons baking powder
2 tablespoons milk,
   at room temperature

Preheat the oven to 180°C (350°F) Gas 4.

Cream the butter and sugar in an electric mixer or with
a handheld electric whisk until pale, light and fluffy, about
2–3 minutes. Very gradually add the beaten eggs, mixing well
between each addition and scraping down the bowl with
a rubber spatula from time to time. Stir in the vanilla extract.

Sift together the plain flour and baking powder and add to the
cake mixture in 2 batches, mixing until smooth. Add the milk
and mix until smooth.

Revert to the relevant cake recipe and continue as instructed.

ALTERNATIVE FLAVOURS

Basic chocolate: substitute 4 tablespoons cocoa for the
same quantity of plain flour in the Extra Large mixture,
3 tablespoons in the Large, 2 in the Medium and 1 in the
Small cake.

Lemon or orange: substitute the grated zest of an unwaxed
lemon or orange for the vanilla extract.

These biscuits will keep un-iced for 3 days in an airtight container. Once iced, they should be eaten within 24 hours.

gingerbread shapes

175 g plain flour
¼ teaspoon bicarbonate
   of soda
a pinch of salt
1 rounded teaspoon
   ground ginger
1 teaspoon ground
   cinnamon
a large pinch of ground
   allspice
75 g unsalted butter,
   cold and diced
75 g caster sugar
2 rounded tablespoons
   golden syrup
1 large egg yolk

*several baking trays, lined
   with baking parchment*

MAKES ABOUT 10–12

Sift the flour, bicarbonate of soda, salt, ginger, cinnamon and allspice into a bowl or an electric free-standing mixer.

Rub the butter into the dry ingredients (or process) until the mixture resembles breadcrumbs. Add the sugar and mix.

Beat the golden syrup and egg yolk together, add to the bowl and mix to a smooth dough, kneading very lightly.

Flatten into a disc, cover with clingfilm and refrigerate for 30 minutes before using.

Preheat the oven to 180°C (350°F) Gas 4.

On a lightly floured work surface, roll the gingerbread dough out to a thickness of about 4 mm. Stamp out your desired shapes and arrange on the prepared baking trays. Re-roll and stamp out any trimmings.

Bake on the middle shelf of the preheated oven for 10–12 minutes until firm and starting to darken very slightly at the edges. Leave to cool slightly on the baking trays, then transfer to a wire cooling rack.

These biscuits will keep un-iced for 3 days in an airtight container. Once iced, they should be eaten within 24 hours.

shortbread

225 g unsalted butter,
    at room temperature
275 g caster sugar
1 large egg, beaten
½ teaspoon vanilla extract
a pinch of salt

325 g plain flour

*several baking trays, lined
    with baking parchment*

MAKES ABOUT 10–12

Cream the butter and sugar in an electric mixer or with a handheld electric whisk until pale, light and fluffy, about 2–3 minutes. Add the beaten egg, vanilla extract and a pinch of salt and mix until combined.

Gradually add the flour and mix until incorporated. Flatten the dough into a disc, cover with clingfilm and refrigerate for a couple of hours before using.

On a lightly floured work surface, roll the shortbread dough out to a thickness of about 4 mm. Stamp out your desired shapes and arrange on the prepared baking trays. Re-roll and stamp out any trimmings. Refrigerate for a further 15 minutes.

Preheat the oven to 180°C (350°F) Gas 4.

Bake on the middle shelf of the preheated oven for 10–12 minutes until pale golden and firm to the touch. Leave to cool slightly on the baking trays, then transfer to a wire cooling rack.

Buttercream is a dream to pipe and spread over cakes of any shape, while chocolate fudge frosting is good enough to eat straight from the bowl! When using meringue frosting it helps to freeze the cake base for 1 hour before icing. This makes the surface of the cake firmer and crumbs are less likely to spoil the clean, white finish of the frosting. Once the frosting has been cooked, work quickly to cover the cake using a palette knife dipped in hot water to make spreading easier. Glacé icing is ideal for decorating gingerbread or shortbread. I use an egg white to make it set firmly but you can use cold water instead (but beware that the icing will not set as stiffly).

buttercream

350 g unsalted butter,
at room temperature
700 g icing sugar, sifted
vanilla extract, optional

Cream the butter in an electric mixer or in a large bowl with a handheld electric whisk until really soft. Gradually beat in the icing sugar until pale and smooth. Add a few drops of vanilla extract, if using.

chocolate fudge frosting

350 g dark chocolate,
   roughly chopped
225 g unsalted butter
225 ml milk
1 teaspoon vanilla extract
450 g icing sugar, sifted

Melt the chocolate and butter together in a heatproof bowl set over a pan of barely simmering water (do not let the base of the bowl touch the water). Stir until melted and smooth, then set aside to cool slightly.

In another bowl, whisk together the milk, vanilla extract and icing sugar until smooth. Add the cooled chocolate mixture and stir until smooth. Leave the frosting to set and thicken up slightly before use.

meringue frosting

250 g caster sugar
4 large egg whites
a pinch of salt

Set a medium-large heatproof bowl over a pan of barely simmering water (do not let the base of the bowl touch the water). Put the sugar, egg whites, salt and 2 tablespoons water into the bowl and using a handheld electric whisk, whisk on medium speed so that the sugar completely dissolves into the egg whites. Continue to whisk until the meringue is white, soft and pillowy. Increase the speed to high and whisk for another minute until the meringue is hot, stiff and glossy.

Remove from the heat and continue whisking for a further minute until the meringue has cooled slightly. Working very quickly and using a palette knife dipped in hot water, spread the frosting over the cake.

glacé icing

1 large egg white
1 tablespoon freshly
   squeezed lemon juice
250–300 g icing sugar,
   sifted

Beat the egg white with the lemon juice in a medium bowl until combined. Gradually add the icing sugar until the icing is smooth and the consistency of slightly thickened double cream and will coat the back of a spoon. Keep covered with clingfilm until ready to use.

decoration

SUGAR PASTE (REGAL ICE) AND ROYAL ICING
Sugar paste (Regal Ice) and royal icing are ideal for modelling and cutting into decorative shapes. They are available ready-to-roll – simply follow the manufacturer's instructions. They can be found in white in many supermarkets, but for a wider range of colours, go to a specialist shop.

FONDANT ICING
Fondant icing is also readily available and sold in blocks. It requires rolling out on a work surface that has been lightly dusted with icing sugar. Use food colouring pastes to tint the icing to your desired shade. Once iced, cover the cake and leave it for at least 4 hours to allow the icing to dry.

READY-ROLLED ICING
Ready-rolled royal and fondant icing can easily be found in most supermarkets' home baking sections and usually come in a circle ready for icing a round cake. I would suggest covering the cake first in a thin layer of either buttercream or marzipan.

WRITING ICING

Ready-to-use writing icing tubes are widely available in the baking sections of most supermarkets and come in a selection of colours but mainly red, green, black and yellow. They are ideal when small amounts of icing are required for writing letters, numbers and words on cakes and for drawing outlines. They are small and easy for children to use without getting too messy! Look out for gel and sparkly writing icing too.

PIPING BAGS

Even if your icing skills aren't in the professional league, a piping bag and selection of nozzles are useful for creating simple but effective decorations. Fit a piping bag with a star-shaped nozzle and fill with buttercream to create rosette or flower shapes as a simple way of covering cakes.

TINTING WITH FOOD COLOURING

Food colouring pastes are easier to use than the standard liquid colours and come in a vast selection of colours. They can be used to tint ready-to-roll icing, fondant icing and buttercream, and are generally available from cake decorating supply shops and online suppliers. A very tiny amount gives a good colour without watering down the icing. Add the paste very gradually using the point of a cocktail stick or wooden skewer and mix well or knead into the icing before adding more until you have the shade you're after.

SPRINKLES AND SWEETS

Most supermarkets carry a wide range of edible decorating sprinkles in the home baking section, ranging from hundreds and thousands to edible silver balls and shapes especially for Halloween and Christmas. Specialist cake decorating shops generally stock a wide range of sprinkles in many shapes and colours. Sweet shops are a fantastic source for cake decorations – liquorice shapes, chocolate buttons, sugar-coated chocolate drops and marshmallows can all be used to great effect on cakes.

basic techniques

1 CUTTING

Always use a long-bladed, serrated knife to slice cakes into layers for filling. Put the cake on a clean, flat work surface. Hold the knife level and horizontal and use a gentle sawing action to slice the cake evenly. Keep your fingers out of the way!

2 FILLING

Cakes can be filled with a variety of fillings such as buttercream, jam, or whipped fresh cream. If necessary, cut a thin slice off the top of the cakes to make the surfaces flat. Lay the bottom layer on the work surface or serving plate and spoon the filling on to the cake. Spread evenly using a long palette knife. Top with another layer of cake and repeat as necessary.

3 CUTTING THE CAKE BASE FOR THE PIRATE SHIP (PAGE 74)

Lay the cake on the work surface with the long edge closest to you. Trim the edges of the cake to make a neat rectangle and save any trimmings to snack on. Using a long-bladed knife, cut a rectangle, about 9 x 23 cm, from one end of the cake. Slice the remaining cake in half to give 2 rectangles roughly 11 x 23 cm.

4 STACKING THE PIECES OF CAKE FOR THE PIRATE SHIP

Stack the 2 larger rectangles one on top of the other. Cut the small rectangle in half and lay one piece at each end of the stacked cakes.

5   6   7   8

5 SHAPING THE PIECES OF CAKE FOR THE PIRATE SHIP

Slice a triangular wedge from the front of the cake, on both sides, to make the prow of the pirate ship. Once you have the cake cut and assembled you can secure the sections with wooden skewers or brush a little warmed jam between the layers to stick them together. The pirate ship is now ready to be iced. Remember to pull out any skewers before serving the cake.

6 PAPER TEMPLATES

Draw or trace your desired shape on to a sheet of paper (for example greaseproof paper or baking parchment) the same size as your uncut cake. Lay the template on the cake and, using a small, sharp knife, cut around the template. This is easier if the cake has been make the day before and if possible chilled in the fridge for a couple of hours first.

7 ICING

When icing a cake that has been cut out from a template, refrigerate the cake for 1–2 hours first. Alternatively, you can brush the surface of the cake with a little warmed, sieved jam first. This helps prevent crumbs mixing into the frosting as you spread it over the cut edges. A selection of palette knives in different sizes is useful. I often use small palette knives bought from artists' supply shops for the trickier shapes.

8 PIPING DECORATION

Once your cake has been covered in frosting, the fun starts! With a steady hand, pipe outlines on to the frosting to clearly define the shapes which can later be filled in with another colour of frosting. Have a clear idea of exactly where you want to draw the lines before starting. You may find it easier to mark out the lines using the point of a cocktail stick first.

diagrams

MARMALADE CAT

JOLLY GREEN DINOSAUR

BUNNY RABBIT

FIRE ENGINE

ROCKET SHIP

HOT AIR BALLOON

BIG GREEN TRACTOR

FAIRYTALE CASTLE

STEAM TRAIN SET

simple cakes

This cake keeps really well and can be made a day in advance and kept un-iced either wrapped in clingfilm or in an airtight container until ready to serve.

carrot & coconut cake

75 g shelled pecan nuts
375 g plain flour
2 teaspoons baking powder
1 teaspoon bicarbonate
   of soda
½ teaspoon ground cinnamon
3 large eggs
375 ml groundnut or
   sunflower oil
450 g unrefined caster sugar
4 tablespoons milk
1 teaspoon vanilla extract
500 g carrots, grated
grated zest of 1 orange
125 g desiccated coconut
100 g marzipan
orange food colouring paste
angelica

FROSTING
450 g cream cheese
2–3 rounded tablespoons
   clear honey

*2 x 20-cm round springform
   cake tins, greased and
   base-lined with greased
   baking parchment*

SERVES 8–10

Preheat the oven to 180°C (350°F) Gas 4.

Put the pecan nuts on a baking tray and toast in the preheated oven for 7 minutes. Leave to cool slightly, then roughly chop. Leave the oven on.

Sift the flour, baking powder, bicarbonate of soda and cinnamon together into a bowl and set aside.

In another bowl, whisk together the eggs, groundnut oil, sugar, milk and vanilla extract and mix until smooth. Add the carrots, orange zest, desiccated coconut and pecan nuts and mix well. Add the dry ingredients and fold in using a large spoon or rubber spatula until thoroughly combined.

Divide the mixture between the prepared cake tins and bake on the middle shelf of the preheated oven for about 40 minutes, or until a skewer inserted into the middle of the cakes comes out clean. Leave the cakes to cool in

the tins for 10 minutes before turning out on to wire cooling racks. Turn the cakes the right way up and leave to cool completely.

To make the frosting, beat the cream cheese and honey together until smooth. Place one of the carrot cakes on a large plate and spread half the frosting over the it. Cover with the second cake and the remaining frosting.

To make the carrots, tint the marzipan orange with the orange food colouring paste (page 17). Break off ½–1 teaspoon marzipan and roll between your hands into a carrot shape. Repeat with the remaining marzipan. Using the blunt end of a wooden skewer push a small hole into the top of each carrot. Leave the carrots to dry overnight on a sheet of baking parchment in an airtight container.

Cut the angelica into very fine matchsticks about 2 cm long and push into the top of each carrot. Decorate the cake with the carrots and an optional chocolate rabbit!

Banoffee pie in a cake! Dulce de leche is a hugely popular ingredient in Argentinian desserts and sweets. It is now widely available in most supermarkets and is sometimes called Banoffee Toffee.

banana & toffee cake

325 g plain flour

1½ teaspoons baking powder

1 teaspoon bicarbonate of soda

3 ripe bananas

4 tablespoons soured cream or crème fraîche, at room temperature

1 teaspoon vanilla extract

175 g unsalted butter, at room temperature

125 g soft light brown sugar

100 g caster sugar

4 large eggs, beaten

100 g dark chocolate, grated

FROSTING

400 g mascarpone

400 g dulce de leche

2 x 20-cm round springform cake tins, greased and base-lined with greased baking parchment

SERVES 10

Preheat the oven to 180°C (350°F) Gas 4.

Sift the flour, baking powder and bicarbonate of soda together into a bowl and set aside.

Mash the bananas in a bowl and mix in the soured cream and vanilla extract.

Cream the butter and sugar in an electric mixer or with a handheld electric whisk until pale, light and fluffy. Gradually add the eggs, mixing well between each addition and scraping down the bowl with a rubber spatula from time to time.

Add the dry ingredients in 2 or 3 batches with the mixer or whisk on a slow speed, mixing well until thoroughly incorporated. Fold in the banana mixture using a rubber spatula.

Divide the mixture between the prepared cake tins and bake on the middle shelf of the preheated oven for about 35 minutes, or until a skewer inserted into the middle of the cakes comes out clean. Leave the cakes to cool in the tins for 10 minutes before turning out on to wire cooling racks. Turn the cakes the right way up and leave to cool completely.

When you are ready to assemble the cake, take a large, serrated knife and slice each cake in half horizontally to give 4 even layers.

Place one cake layer on a serving plate and spread with one-quarter of the mascarpone. Carefully spread or drizzle one-quarter of the dulce de leche over the mascarpone followed by one-quarter of the grated chocolate. Continue layering up in this manner, ending with a layer of chocolate.

This cake keeps really well wrapped in clingfilm or in an airtight container and can be made a day in advance and iced on the day of the party. Don't be tempted to over-swirl the mixtures or the marble effect will be less dramatic.

marble cake

75 g dark chocolate,
    roughly chopped
175 g plain flour
1 slightly rounded teaspoon
    baking powder
175 g unsalted butter,
    at room temperature
200 g caster sugar
1 teaspoon vanilla extract
4 large eggs, beaten
assorted chocolate
    sprinkles

FROSTING
125 g dark chocolate
75 g unsalted butter
75 ml milk
½ teaspoon vanilla extract
150 g icing sugar

20 x 13-cm loaf tin, greased
and the base and ends
lined with a strip of
greased baking
parchment

SERVES 8–10

Preheat the oven to 180°C (350°F) Gas 4.

Put the chocolate in a heatproof bowl set over a pan of barely simmering water (do not let the base of the bowl touch the water). Stir until melted and smooth, then set aside to cool slightly.

Sift the flour and baking powder together.

Cream the butter and sugar in an electric mixer or with a handheld electric whisk until pale, light and fluffy. Stir in the vanilla extract. Gradually add the eggs, mixing well between each addition and scraping down the bowl with a rubber spatula from time to time.

Add the dry ingredients and mix until smooth. Spoon one-third of the mixture into the melted chocolate. Mix until smooth.

Using a tablespoon, drop alternate spoonfuls of vanilla and chocolate mixture into the prepared loaf tin. Once all of the mixture has been used, give the tin a sharp tap on the work surface to level the mixture. To create a marble effect, drag the blade of a table knife through the mixture to create swirls, taking care not to over-swirl the mixture.

Bake on the middle shelf of the preheated oven for about 1 hour, or until a skewer inserted into the middle of the cake comes out clean. Leave the cake to cool in the tin for 10 minutes before turning out on to a wire cooling rack. Turn the cake the right way up and leave to cool completely.

To make the frosting, put the chocolate and butter in a heatproof bowl set over a pan of barely simmering water (do not let the base of the bowl touch the water). Stir until melted and smooth, then set aside to cool slightly.

In another bowl, whisk together the milk, vanilla extract and icing sugar until smooth. Add the cooled chocolate mixture and stir until smooth. Leave the frosting to set and thicken up slightly before use.

Once the cake is completely cold, ice with the frosting and decorate with your choice of assorted chocolate sprinkles.

This is a deliciously light lemon layer cake. Go wild with the decorations and use lots of different varieties and colours of sweets. The cake can be assembled and iced in advance but don't add the sweets until about 1–2 hours before serving otherwise they will soften and bleed into the frosting.

lemon cake

400 g plain flour
1 tablespoon baking powder
225 g unsalted butter, at room temperature
225 g caster sugar
4 large eggs, beaten
250 ml soured cream, at room temperature
grated zest of 2 unwaxed lemons and freshly squeezed juice of 1
assorted sweets

FROSTING
350 g unsalted butter, at room temperature
600 g icing sugar, sifted
4 tablespoons lemon curd

2 x 20-cm round springform cake tins, greased and base-lined with greased baking parchment

SERVES 8–10

Preheat the oven to 180°C (350°F) Gas 4.

Sift the flour and baking powder together.

Cream the butter and sugar in an electric mixer or with a handheld electric whisk until pale, light and fluffy. Gradually add the eggs, mixing well between each addition and scraping down the bowl with a rubber spatula from time to time.

With the mixer or whisk on a low speed add the dry ingredients and soured cream alternately to the mixture in batches. Add the lemon zest and juice and mix until smooth.

Divide the mixture evenly between the prepared cake tins and bake on the middle shelf of the preheated oven for about 35 minutes, or until a skewer inserted into the middle of the cakes comes out clean. Leave the cakes to cool in the tins for 10 minutes

before turning out on to wire cooling racks. Turn the cakes the right way up and leave to cool completely.

To make the frosting, cream the butter and icing sugar until smooth and pale. Add the lemon curd and mix again until smooth.

When you are ready to assemble the cake, take a large, serrated knife and slice each cake in half horizontally to give 4 even layers.

Place one cake layer on a serving plate and spread with 2 heaped tablespoons of frosting. Top with another cake layer and frosting. Repeat until you have 4 layers of cake and 3 of frosting. Cover the top and sides of the whole cake with the remaining frosting, spreading evenly with a palette knife.

Decorate the cake with your choice of assorted sweets.

This recipe has been adapted from one by Emily Luchetti in her fabulous *Stars Desserts* cookbook which is now sadly out of print. Make the cake in advance and assemble on the day of the party.

fantastic chocolate cake

125 g best-quality cocoa
250 ml boiling water
400 g plain flour
2 teaspoons baking powder
1½ teaspoons bicarbonate
   of soda
150 g unsalted butter,
   at room temperature
500 g unrefined caster sugar
3 large eggs, beaten
300 ml buttermilk,
   at room temperature

FROSTING
350 g dark chocolate,
   roughly chopped
225 g unsalted butter
225 ml milk
1 teaspoon vanilla extract
450 g icing sugar, sifted

*10-cm, 18-cm and 23-cm
round springform cake
tins, greased and base-
lined with greased
baking parchment*

SERVES 14–16

Preheat the oven to 180°C (350°F) Gas 4.

Put the cocoa and boiling water in a medium bowl, whisk until smooth and set aside to cool down.

Sift the flour, baking powder and bicarbonate of soda together into a bowl.

Cream the butter and sugar in an electric mixer or with a handheld electric whisk until pale, light and fluffy. Gradually add the eggs, mixing well between each addition and scraping down the bowl with a rubber spatula from time to time.

Add the dry ingredients and buttermilk alternately to the mixture in batches. Add the cocoa mixture and stir until thoroughly combined and the batter is smooth.

Divide the mixture between the prepared cake tins. Bake in the preheated oven until a skewer inserted into the middle of the cakes comes out clean – about 25 minutes for the smallest cake, 30–35 minutes for the medium cake, and 40–45 minutes for the largest

cake. Leave the cakes to cool in the tins for 10 minutes before turning out on to wire cooling racks. Turn the cakes the right way up and leave to cool completely.

To make the frosting, melt the chocolate and butter in a heatproof bowl set over a pan of barely simmering water (do not let the base of the bowl touch the water). Stir until melted and smooth and set aside to cool slightly.

In another bowl, whisk together the milk, vanilla extract and icing sugar until smooth. Add the cooled chocolate mixture and stir until smooth. Leave the frosting to set and thicken up slightly before using.

Using a long, serrated knife cut all 3 cakes in half horizontally. Place one layer of the largest cake on a serving plate and spread with a couple of tablespoons of the frosting. Cover with the other half of the cake. Repeat with the remaining cakes, stacking one on top of the other, from large to small. Cover the whole cake with frosting, spreading it evenly with a palette knife.

If you don't want to make nine building blocks, this cake can easily be cut into four larger squares instead. Beware that the cake needs to be left overnight before the party (in an airtight container) to give the icing time to set.

building blocks

2 quantities Medium Basic
   Vanilla Sponge (page 11)
6 tablespoons raspberry
   jam, sieved
3 tablespoons Buttercream
   (page 14), optional
500 g marzipan
500 g ready-to-roll
   royal icing
food colouring pastes
   of your choice

2 x 20-cm square
   springform cake tins,
   greased and base-lined
   with greased baking
   parchment
small letter or number
   cutters
ribbons

MAKES 9

Preheat the oven to 180°C (350°F) Gas 4.

Make the 2 quantities of Vanilla Sponge and divide between the prepared cake tins. Bake on the middle shelf of the preheated oven for 35–40 minutes, or until a skewer inserted into the middle of the cakes comes out clean. Leave the cakes to cool in the tins for 10 minutes before turning out on to wire cooling racks. Turn the cakes the right way up and leave to cool completely.

Level off the tops of the cakes with a sharp knife. Sandwich the cakes together with 2 tablespoons each of jam and buttercream, if using. Trim off the edges so that the cake has completely even sides. Cut the cake into 9 blocks. Heat the remaining jam in a small saucepan until runny, sieve, then use to brush the top and sides of each block.

Divide the marzipan into 9 even-sized pieces. Lightly dust the work surface with icing sugar and roll out each piece of marzipan into a square no thicker than 2 mm, and large enough to cover each block. Cover the tops and sides of the blocks with marzipan,

smoothing the surface with icing sugar-dusted hands. Set aside for at least 1 hour.

If using more than one food colouring, divide up the royal icing and tint each portion with your chosen colouring paste(s) (page 17). Remember that you need 9 equal pieces of icing at the end to cover your blocks. Cover with clingfilm whichever icing you're not about to use. Cut the remaining icing into your chosen number of even-sized pieces. Lightly dust the work surface with icing sugar and roll each piece of icing into a square no thicker than 2 mm, and large enough to cover each whole block. Very lightly brush each block with cooled boiled water. Cover the tops and sides of the blocks with the icing, smoothing the surface with icing sugar-dusted hands. Trim off the excess. Repeat with any other coloured icing and remaining blocks.

Thinly roll out the last of the icing and use to stamp out letters or numbers. Very lightly brush with cold water and stick to the sides and top of each cake. Leave the cakes to dry overnight before decorating with ribbons.

Keep any leftovers from the trimmings of this cake and use in a trifle or for popping into lunchboxes. When you are a more confident baker, try making other numbers.

number '5' cake

2 quantities Large Basic
 Vanilla Sponge (page 11)
1 quantity Buttercream
 (page 14)
blue food colouring paste

23-cm round springform
 cake tin and 20-cm
 square cake tin, greased
 and base-lined with
 greased baking
 parchment
7–8-cm round cutter or
 bowl
piping bag, fitted with
 a star-shaped nozzle

SERVES 12–14

Preheat the oven to 180°C (350°F) Gas 4.

Make the 2 quantities of Vanilla Sponge and divide between the prepared cake tins. Bake on the middle shelf of the preheated oven for 30–35 minutes, or until a skewer inserted into the middle of the cakes comes out clean. Leave the cakes to cool in the tins for 10 minutes before turning out on to wire cooling racks. Turn the cakes the right way up and leave to cool completely.

Level off the tops of the cakes with a sharp knife to make them both the same height. Use the round cutter or small bowl to cut a circle out of the middle of the round cake (you will not need this portion for the finished cake). Imagining the round cake as a clock face, cut out the section that would be 9–12 o'clock and discard.

Trim the edges of the square cake and cut in half to give 2 rectangles, each 10 x 20 cm. Cut one of these pieces into a smaller rectangle of roughly 15 x 10 cm.

Place the round cake at the bottom of a large board with the cut-out section on the left-hand side. Position the larger rectangle as the upward part of the 5 and the smaller piece as the top.

Tint the buttercream your desired shade of blue with the blue food colouring paste (page 17). Cover the whole cake with two-thirds of the buttercream, spreading evenly with a palette knife. Tint the remaining buttercream a contrasting colour and use to pipe rosettes around the edge of the cake.

This is a fool-proof method for making meringues that are slightly chewy in the middle but still crisp on the outside. For the sake of your arms, make the mixture in an electric free-standing mixer because it takes 10 minutes for the meringue to become really stiff and glossy. The cooked meringues will keep for 3–4 days in an airtight container.

meringue mountain

300 g caster sugar
150 g egg whites (from
    about 5 large eggs)
pink food colouring paste
blue food colouring paste
edible silver balls and
    coloured sprinkles
1 tablespoon cocoa

*2 solid baking trays, lined
    with baking parchment*

MAKES 12

Preheat the oven to 200°C (400°F) Gas 6.

Tip the sugar into a small roasting tin and warm in the preheated oven for about 7 minutes, or until hot to the touch. Turn the oven down to 110°C (225°F) Gas ¼.

Meanwhile, whisk the egg whites in an electric free-standing mixer until frothy. Tip all of the hot sugar on to the egg whites in one go and continue to mix on high speed for about 10 minutes until the meringue mixture is very stiff, white and cold.

Divide the mixture between 3 bowls. Add tiny amounts of pink food colouring paste to one bowl using a cocktail stick and very gently fold in using a large metal spoon until the colour has marbled the meringue.

Using 2 tablespoons, dollop the meringue into 4 even-sized mounds on to the prepared baking trays. Repeat with the blue food colouring paste.

Sift the cocoa into the last bowl of meringue and gently fold in until the meringue is marbled with cocoa.

Sprinkle edible silver balls and coloured sprinkles all over the meringues, then bake in the preheated oven for 1½–1¾ hours. Remove from the oven and leave to cool on the baking trays. Pile up on a serving plate.

Everyone loves a cupcake. You can go as pretty or as crazy as you like with the icing and decorations on these little treats. Get the birthday girl to help you decorate.

princess cupcakes

1 quantity Large Basic
   Vanilla Sponge (page 11)
1 quantity Buttercream
   (page 14)
food colouring pastes of
   your choice
coloured sprinkles

*piping bags, fitted with
   star-shaped nozzles*
*2 x 12-hole muffin trays,
   lined with 18–20 paper
   cupcake cases*

MAKES 18–20

Preheat the oven to 180°C (350°F) Gas 4.

Make the Vanilla Sponge and divide between the cupcake cases. Bake on the middle shelf of the preheated oven for 20–25 minutes, or until a skewer inserted into the middle of the cupcakes comes out clean. Leave the cupcakes to cool in the trays for 10 minutes before turning out on to a wire cooling rack. Turn the cupcakes the right way up and leave to cool completely.

Divide the buttercream between 3 or 4 bowls, depending how many shades of food colouring you are planning to use. Tint each bowl your desired colour (page 17).

Fill the piping bags with your coloured buttercream and pipe generous swirls of it on top of each cupcake. Decorate with sprinkles and serve on a tiered stand.

Look out for ice cream cone cups that have flat bottoms and will stand upright in the muffin trays while baking. Tint the buttercream pink for strawberry ice cream and scatter with sliced fresh strawberries or a couple of fresh cherries. These cupcakes are best made on the day of the party.

'ice cream' cupcakes

125 g unsalted butter,
  at room temperature
125 g caster sugar
2 large eggs, beaten
1 teaspoon vanilla extract
125 g plain flour
1½ teaspoons baking
  powder
2 tablespoons milk,
  at room temperature
10 ice cream cone cups
  (with flat bottoms)
10 flaked chocolate bars

BUTTERCREAM
250 g unsalted butter,
  at room temperature
500 g icing sugar, sifted
1 teaspoon vanilla extract

12-hole muffin tray
piping bag, fitted with
  a star-shaped nozzle

MAKES 10

Preheat the oven to 180°C (350°F) Gas 4. Stand the ice cream cones in the muffin tray.

Cream the butter and sugar in an electric mixer or with a handheld electric whisk until pale, light and fluffy. Gradually add the eggs, mixing well between each addition and scraping down the bowl with a rubber spatula from time to time. Stir in the vanilla extract.

Sift the flour and baking powder together, then fold into the creamed mixture. Add the milk and stir until smooth. Divide the mixture between the ice cream cones and bake on the middle shelf of the preheated oven for 20–25 minutes until golden and a skewer inserted in the middle of the cupcakes comes out clean. Leave the cupcakes to cool in the muffin tray for 10 minutes before turning out on to a wire cooling rack to cool completely.

To make the buttercream, cream the butter, sugar and vanilla extract as above. Fill the piping bag with the buttercream and pipe generous swirls of it on top of each cupcake. Finish with a flaked chocolate bar.

This is the perfect birthday cake as it can be made 3 days in advance, kept covered in the freezer, then decorated with the chopped mints just before serving.

ice cream layer cake

175 g caster sugar

3 large egg whites

1 quantity Medium Basic Chocolate Sponge (page 11)

1 litre good-quality vanilla ice cream

1.5 litres good-quality chocolate ice cream

200 g chocolate mint matchsticks or chocolate bittermints, chopped

mint humbugs or similar, roughly chopped

33 x 23 x 6-cm cake tin, greased and lined with greased baking parchment

SERVES 12

Preheat the oven to 200°C (400°F) Gas 6.

Tip the sugar into a small roasting tin and warm in the preheated oven for about 5 minutes. Turn the oven down to 110°C (225°F) Gas ¼.

Meanwhile, whisk the egg whites in an electric mixer until frothy. Tip all of the hot sugar on to the egg whites in one go and continue to mix on high speed for about 8 minutes until the meringue mixture is very stiff, white and cold.

Spoon into the prepared cake tin, spread level using a palette knife and cook on the middle shelf of the oven for 1½ hours, or until the surface is crisp. Remove from the oven and leave in the tin to cool completely. When cold, remove from the tin and clean the tin, ready for baking the cake layers.

To make the cake layers, grease the cake tin and base-line with greased baking parchment. Preheat the oven to 180°C (350°F) Gas 4.

Make the Chocolate Sponge and spoon into the prepared cake tin. Bake on the middle shelf of the preheated oven for 20–25 minutes. Leave the cake to cool in the tin for 10 minutes before turning out on to a wire cooling rack. Turn the cake the right way up and leave to cool completely.

To assemble the cake you will need the vanilla ice cream and one-quarter of the chocolate ice cream to be soft so transfer them to the fridge for 20 minutes.

Using a long, serrated knife cut the cake in half to give 2 smaller rectangles roughly 23 x 16 cm. Carefully remove the baking parchment from the meringue and cut the meringue in the same way.

Tip the vanilla ice cream into a bowl and stir through the chocolate mint matchsticks.

Working quickly, place one cake layer on a board and spread with half the vanilla ice cream. Top this with a layer of meringue. Spread the chocolate ice cream over the meringue and cover with the remaining meringue layer. Spread with the remaining vanilla ice cream and the remaining chocolate cake. Cover the cake with clingfilm and place in the freezer on rapid freeze for at least 2 hours or until solid. Transfer to a serving plate and neaten the edges with a long knife.

Allow the remaining chocolate ice cream to soften slightly in the fridge for 20 minutes, then use to spread all over the top and sides of the cake. Freeze again for about 1 hour.

When you are ready to serve the cake, scatter the top with the mint humbugs.

If you don't like marzipan, you can spread a layer of buttercream over the cake before covering it with the icing. Beware that the cake needs to be left overnight (in an airtight container) to give the icing time to set.

snakes & ladders

1 quantity Extra Large Basic
   Vanilla Sponge (page 11)
6 tablespoons apricot or
   raspberry jam
750 g marzipan
1 kg ready-to-roll
   fondant icing
green food colouring paste
yellow food colouring paste
black writing icing
assorted jelly snakes

*25.5-cm square cake tin,
   greased and base-lined
   with greased baking
   parchment*
ribbon (optional)

SERVES 15–20

Preheat the oven to 180°C (350°F) Gas 4.

Make the Vanilla Sponge and spoon into the prepared cake tin. Bake on the middle shelf of the preheated oven for 40–45 minutes, or until a skewer inserted into the middle of the cake comes out clean. Leave the cake to cool in the tin for 10 minutes before turning out on to a wire cooling rack. Turn the cake the right way up and leave to cool completely.

Level off the top of the cake with a sharp knife if necessary. Place the cake on a serving plate.

Heat the jam in a small saucepan until runny, sieve, then use to brush the top and sides of the cake.

Lightly dust the work surface with icing sugar and roll the marzipan out to a square slightly larger than the cake. Cover the top and sides of the cake with marzipan, smoothing the surface with icing sugar-dusted hands and trimming off any excess. Set aside for at least 1 hour.

Lightly brush the marzipan with a little cooled boiled water.

Lightly dust the work surface with icing sugar and roll three-quarters of the icing out to a square slightly larger than the cake. Cover the top and sides of the cake with icing, smoothing the surface with icing sugar-dusted hands and trimming off any excess.

Divide the remaining icing into 2 even portions and tint one half yellow and the other green (page 17). Thinly roll out and cut into even-sized squares to make a chequerboard pattern on top of the cake. Stick in place with a little cooled boiled water. Set aside to dry overnight in an airtight container.

The next day, use the writing icing to draw numbers and ladders on the squares. Tie a ribbon, if using, around the bottom of the cake and decorate with an assortment of jelly snakes.

Bake the cake base the day before you plan to ice these fondant fancies and store in an airtight container overnight – this makes them easier to cut and ice. These little cakes are perfect for just a couple of mouthfuls.

fondant fancies

150 g unsalted butter,
   at room temperature
150 g caster sugar
2 large eggs, beaten
150 g plain flour
2 teaspoons baking powder
3–4 tablespoons milk,
   at room temperature
50 g ground almonds
grated zest and freshly
   squeezed juice of
   ½ unwaxed lemon
2 tablespoons lemon curd
1 tablespoon apricot jam
100 g marzipan
sugar flowers
edible silver balls

ICING
500 g fondant icing sugar
freshly squeezed juice of
   1 lemon
pink food colouring paste

*20-cm square cake tin,
   greased and base-lined
   with greased baking
   parchment*
*piping bag, fitted with
   a small, plain nozzle*

MAKES ABOUT 16

Preheat the oven to 180°C (350°F) Gas 4.

Cream the butter and sugar in an electric mixer or with a handheld electric whisk until pale, light and fluffy. Gradually add the eggs, mixing well between each addition and scraping down the bowl with a rubber spatula from time to time.

Sift the flour and baking powder together, then fold half into the creamed mixture followed by half the milk. Add the remaining flour and milk in alternate batches.

Fold in the ground almonds, lemon zest and juice, stir until smooth, then spoon into the prepared cake tin. Bake on the middle shelf of the preheated oven for 25–30 minutes, or until a skewer inserted into the middle of the cake comes out clean. Leave the cake to cool in the tin for 10 minutes before turning out on to a wire cooling rack. Leave to cool, then store in an airtight container overnight.

The next day, level off the top of the cake with a sharp knife if necessary. Cut the cake in half horizontally. Place the bottom cake layer on a board and spread the cut surface with the lemon curd. Cover with the other cake layer, cut side down.

Heat the jam in a small saucepan until runny, sieve, then use to brush the top of the cake.

Lightly dust the work surface with icing sugar and roll the marzipan out to a square the same size as the cake, using the cake tin as a guide. Lay the marzipan on top of the jam, smoothing the surface with icing sugar-dusted hands. Trim the sides of the cake, then cut into neat 4-cm cubes.

Mix the fondant icing sugar with lemon juice until it is smooth and thick enough to coat the cakes. Transfer half the icing to a small bowl, add pink food colouring to your desired shade (page 17) and cover with clingfilm. Colour the remaining icing a different shade of pink. Coat the top and sides of each cake in the 2 colours of fondant icing and leave to dry on a cooling rack. (The easiest way to do this is to hold one cake on a fork over the bowl and drizzle the icing over the top and sides to coat evenly.) Set aside any leftover icing and cover with clingfilm. Transfer the cakes to a cooling rack and leave for at least 1 hour or until set.

Fill the piping bag with the remaining fondant icing and pipe thin lines and dots on each cake. Decorate with sugar flowers and edible silver balls. Leave to dry before serving.

animals

This is my favourite cake and it's so simple. All of the chocolates used in this recipe are easily found in the supermarket or sweet shop. Look out for chocolate buttons in different sizes.

wise owl

1 quantity Extra Large Basic
    Vanilla or Chocolate
    Sponge (page 11)
1 quantity Chocolate Fudge
    Frosting (page 15)
chocolate buttons in
    different sizes
chocolate vermicelli
1 flaked chocolate bar
1 chocolate-covered
    toffee bar

*2 x 23-cm round springform
    cake tins, greased and
    base-lined with greased
    baking parchment
piping bag, fitted with
    a star-shaped nozzle*

SERVES 12–16

Preheat the oven to 180°C (350°F) Gas 4.

Make the Vanilla Sponge mixture and divide between the prepared cake tins. Bake on the middle shelf of the preheated oven for 30–35 minutes, or until a skewer inserted into the middle of the cakes comes out clean. Leave the cakes to cool in the tins for 10 minutes before turning out on to a wire cooling rack. Turn the cakes the right way up and leave to cool completely.

Level off the tops of the cakes with a sharp knife if necessary. Place one cake on a serving plate and spread the cut surface with about 3 tablespoons of the Chocolate Fudge Frosting. Cover with the other cake layer, cut side down. Cover the top and sides of the whole cake with three-quarters of the

remaining Chocolate Fudge Frosting, spreading evenly with a palette knife.

Arrange the chocolate buttons over the bottom half of the cake to resemble feathers and cover the top half of the cake with chocolate vermicelli. Fill the piping bag with the remaining Chocolate Frosting and use this to pipe feathers around the owl's face.

Position assorted chocolate buttons on top of the sprinkles for the eyes. Cut the flaked chocolate bar into thin pieces and push into the bottom edge of the cake to make legs. Cut the toffee bar in half. Slice one half diagonally into 2 pieces for the wings and push one into each side of the owl. Cut the remaining toffee bar at an angle to make a beak and position on the owl's face.

I have covered this rabbit in meringue frosting but you could use buttercream coloured to your desired shade. For the bunny's tail you only need one cupcake, so freeze the leftovers or turn them into flowers, like those on page 122, and place them around the bunny.

bunny rabbit

1 quantity Extra Large Basic Vanilla Sponge (page 11)
1 quantity Small Basic Vanilla Sponge (page 11)
1 quantity Meringue Frosting (page 15)
pink food colouring paste
2 jelly beans or brown sugar-coated chocolate drops
black writing icing

33 x 23 x 6-cm cake tin, greased and base-lined with greased baking parchment
6-hole muffin tray, lined with paper cases

SERVES 12

Preheat the oven to 180°C (350°F) Gas 4.

Make the Vanilla Sponge mixtures (separately) and spoon the Extra Large into the prepared cake tin and divide the Small between the paper cases. Bake on the middle shelf of the preheated oven until a skewer inserted into the middle of the cakes comes out clean – 40 minutes for the cake and 20–25 minutes for the cupcakes. Leave the cakes to cool in the tin or tray for 10 minutes before turning out on to wire cooling racks. Turn the cakes the right way up and leave to cool completely.

Refer to the diagrams on page 20 and use to draw a similar rabbit shape on a piece of paper. Cut out and lay on top of the cake. Cut around with a sharp knife and use the trimmings to make the head and ears. Arrange the body parts on a large platter.

Take 3–4 tablespoons of the Meringue Frosting for the ears and tail and set aside in a small bowl. Completely cover the top and sides of the rabbit with the Meringue Frosting, peaking the meringue with the back of a spoon so that it looks like fur.

Stir a tiny amount of pink food colouring paste (page 17) into the reserved frosting to make a pale pink. Peel the paper case off one cupcake and cover the cupcake in pink frosting. Fill in the insides of the ears with pink frosting too. Arrange the cupcake on top of the rabbit for the tail.

Position the jelly beans or chocolate drops on the rabbit's face to make an eye and the nose. Using the writing icing, draw whiskers on the face. Set aside for about 1 hour to set slightly before serving.

This cake will appeal to a younger child. Make the cake in advance and assemble on the day of the party. To make the ears and nose you will need to make a batch of cupcakes but since you only need a small number of them for the teddy bear cake, the remaining cupcakes can either be frozen for another time or covered with frosting and served alongside the teddy.

teddy bear

1 quantity Large Basic
    Vanilla or Chocolate
    Sponge (page 11)
1 quantity Small Basic
    Vanilla or Chocolate
    Sponge (page 11)
1 quantity Chocolate Fudge
    Frosting (page 15)
assorted chocolate drops
    and buttons
ribbon

*2 x 20-cm round springform
    cake tins, greased and
    base-lined with greased
    baking parchment
12-hole muffin tray, lined
    with 6 paper cases and 1
    mini paper cupcake case*

SERVES 10

Preheat the oven to 180°C (350°F) Gas 4.

Make the Vanilla Sponge mixtures (separately) and spoon the Large into the prepared cake tins and divide the Small one between the paper cases. Bake on the middle shelf of the preheated oven until a skewer inserted into the middle of the cakes comes out clean – 30 minutes for the cakes, 25 minutes for the cupcakes and 15 minutes for the mini cupcake. Leave all the cakes to cool in the tins or trays for 10 minutes before turning out on to wire cooling racks. Turn the cakes the right way up and leave to cool completely.

Use a long, serrated knife to level the tops of the cakes if necessary. Place one cake on a serving plate and spread 3–4 tablespoons of Chocolate Frosting over the top. Top with the second cake. Use three-quarters of the remaining Chocolate Frosting to cover the top and sides of the whole cake, spreading evenly with a palette knife.

Peel the paper case off one cupcake and cut the cupcake in half horizontally. Position one half on each side of the head to make the ears. Cover the tops of 2 other cupcakes with frosting and place on top of the halved cupcakes so that they are roughly level with the top of the teddy's face.

Peel the paper case off the mini cupcake and completely cover the cupcake with frosting. Position in the middle of the cake to make the teddy's nose. Arrange the chocolate drops on the face for the eyes, mouth and ears. Make a bow out of the ribbon and place at the teddy's neck.

These funny cupcakes look tricky but are actually very simple to make. The only fancy equipment you'll need is a couple of piping bags, nozzles and a steady hand. The cupcakes can be made ahead and stored, un-iced, in the freezer in plastic containers.

animal face cupcakes

1 quantity Large Basic
   Vanilla Sponge (page 11)
1 quantity Buttercream
   (page 14)
brown food colouring paste
black food colouring paste
2 small liquorice sweets
12 sugar-coated chocolate
   drops
black writing icing

*3 piping bags, fitted with
   star-shaped nozzles*
*12-hole muffin tray, lined
   with paper cupcake cases*
*12-hole mini cupcake tray,
   lined with mini paper
   cupcake cases*

MAKES 12

Preheat the oven to 180°C (350°F) Gas 4.

Make the Vanilla Sponge mixture and use to fill each cupcake case with a rounded tablespoon, and the mini cases with a rounded teaspoonful. Bake on the middle shelf of the preheated oven – the cupcakes will take 20–25 minutes and the mini cupcakes will take 10–15 minutes. A skewer inserted into the middle of the cakes should come out clean. Leave to cool in the trays for 10 minutes, then transfer to a wire rack to cool completely.

Divide the buttercream between 3 bowls and tint one brown and one grey with the brown and black food colouring pastes (page 17) and leave the third plain.

Fill the piping bags with the coloured buttercreams. Pipe lines of buttercream on top of the cupcakes, from the outside to the centre in a slight dome – cover 4 of the cupcakes with brown buttercream, 4 with grey, and 4 with white. Repeat with the mini cupcakes, making ears at the top of each cake.

Cut the liquorice into tiny pieces for noses and position one on each mini cupcake. Cut the chocolate drops in half and position on the ears. Using the black writing icing, pipe eyes and whiskers onto each mini cupcake. Position the mini cakes at an angle on top of the cupcakes and push gently until they are firmly stuck in place.

This is guaranteed to appeal to the dinosaur-loving birthday boy or girl. Look out for chocolate-coated wafers in the biscuit aisle of the supermarket as they make ideal spines. Garnish the serving plate with chocolate-coated 'boulders'.

jolly green dinosaur

1 quantity Extra Large Basic
   Vanilla Sponge (page 11)
1 quantity Buttercream
   (page 14)
green food colouring paste
brown food colouring paste
14 mini chocolate drops
chocolate-coated wafers
green diamond-shaped
   sweets
chocolate sprinkles
green sprinkles
2 white chocolate buttons
black writing icing

*2 x 23-cm round springform
   cake tins, greased and
   base-lined with greased
   baking parchment
piping bag, fitted with
   a star-shaped nozzle*

SERVES 10–12

Preheat the oven to 180°C (350°F) Gas 4.

Make the Vanilla Sponge mixture and divide between the prepared cake tins. Bake on the middle shelf of the preheated oven for 35–40 minutes, or until a skewer inserted into the middle of the cakes comes out clean. Leave the cakes to cool in the tins for 10 minutes before turning out on to wire cooling racks. Leave to cool completely, then store overnight in an airtight container.

The next day, assemble the dinosaur (refer to the diagrams on page 20). Use a long, serrated knife to level the tops of the cakes if necessary. Lay the cakes one on top of the other, cut sides facing each other. Cut the bottom third off both cakes and reserve. Separate the cakes again and spread some of the buttercream over one cut side. Sandwich the 2 cakes together, then place upright (resting on the flat side) in the middle of a serving plate.

The reserved pieces of cake should look like orange segments. Take one segment and cut it in half to make 2 rough triangle shapes. Sandwich the 2 shapes together with a little buttercream and position upright as the head of the dinosaur. Cut 4 strips from the straight side of the remaining segment and stick 2 strips with buttercream on each side of the dinosaur to make each leg. You should have a slim segment shape leftover. Cut this in half to make 2 rough triangle shapes. Sandwich the 2 shapes together with a little buttercream and position upright as the tail.

Reserve 4 tablespoons of the buttercream in a small bowl. Tint the remaining buttercream green with the green food colouring paste (page 17). Fill a piping bag with the green buttercream and use to cover the dinosaur with rosettes. Tint the reserved buttercream brown and pipe little feet on to the legs. Press on the mini chocolate buttons for the claws.

Push the chocolate-coated wafers all down the back of the dinosaur to make scales and position the green jelly diamonds in between each wafer. Scatter the chocolate and green sprinkles all over the dinosaur. Stick the white chocolate buttons on the face for the eyes and use the black writing icing for the centre of the eyes and to make a mouth. Position the last mini chocolate buttons as nostrils.

For this recipe you need only one cupcake, but if you make a batch, the remaining cupcakes can either be frozen for use another time or iced and served alongside the hedgehog. You could even buy extra matchsticks and make the cupcakes into baby hedgehogs!

prickly hedgehog

1 quantity Large Basic
　　Vanilla or Chocolate
　　Sponge (page 11)
1 quantity Small Basic
　　Vanilla or Chocolate
　　Sponge (page 11)
1 quantity Chocolate Fudge
　　Frosting (page 15)
chocolate vermicelli
about 500 g chocolate mint
　　matchsticks
3 chocolate drops

*2-litre ovenproof glass
　　bowl, greased and
　　dusted with flour*
*6-hole muffin tray, lined
　　with paper cases*

SERVES 10

Preheat the oven to 180°C (350°F) Gas 4.

Make the Vanilla Sponge mixtures (separately) and spoon the Large into the prepared bowl and divide the Small between the paper cases. Bake on the middle shelf of the preheated oven until a skewer inserted into the middle of the cakes comes out clean – 1 hour for the cake and 20–25 minutes for the cupcakes. Leave the cakes to cool in the bowl or tray for 10 minutes before turning out on to wire cooling racks to cool completely.

Use a long, serrated knife to level the bottom of the cake if necessary. Cut the cake into 3 even horizontal layers. Sandwich the cake together with 3 tablespoons of Chocolate Fudge Frosting between each layer.

Place the cake on a serving plate and cover it with Chocolate Frosting, spreading evenly with a palette knife.

Peel the paper case off one cupcake and level off the domed top. Turn upside down and cover the top and sides with frosting. Scatter with the chocolate vermicelli and position on the plate next to the larger cake for the head.

To make the spines, cut the matchsticks in half and push them into the body of the hedgehog until it is totally covered. Push the chocolate drops into the head for eyes.

This is a very simple cake to make and assemble and can be easily baked on the day of the party. You only need one cupcake so freeze the rest for another time.

fluffy sheep

1 quantity Large Basic Vanilla Sponge (page 11)

1 quantity Small Basic Vanilla Sponge (page 11)

1 quantity Buttercream (page 14)

600 g white mini marshmallows

2 pink regular marshmallows

chocolate vermicelli

2 chocolate drops

black writing icing

2-litre ovenproof glass bowl, greased and dusted with flour

6-hole muffin tray, lined with paper cases

4 cocktail sticks

SERVES ABOUT 10

Preheat the oven to 180°C (350°F) Gas 4.

Make the Vanilla Sponge mixtures (separately) and spoon the Large into the prepared bowl and divide the Small between the paper cases. Bake on the middle shelf of the preheated oven until a skewer inserted into the middle of the cake comes out clean – 1 hour for the cake and 20–25 minutes for the cupcakes. Leave the cakes to cool in the bowl or tray for 10 minutes before turning out on to wire cooling racks to cool completely.

Use a long, serrated knife to level the bottom of the cake if necessary. Put the cake, flat side down, on a serving plate and cover it with buttercream, spreading evenly with a palette knife.

Peel the paper case off one cupcake (and freeze the rest of the cupcakes). Cover the cupcake with buttercream, position on top of the sheep for the head and secure in place with a cocktail stick.

Cover the body and the head of the sheep with the mini marshmallows, leaving a space for the sheep's face. Carefully coat a regular marshmallow with buttercream and stick to the face. Secure in place with a cocktail stick.

Cover the face and nose with chocolate vermicelli and press to stick.

Cut the remaining regular marshmallow in half, pinch the ends together to make ear shapes and attach to the sides of the head with cocktail sticks.

Using the black writing icing, pipe a nose and mouth on the face and use to attach chocolate drop eyes.

The cake quantity used in this recipe is enough to make the body and head of the dog and 8 mini cupcakes. You will only need one cupcake for the finished dog and the remaining cupcakes can be frozen for another time.

mungo the dog

1 quantity Large Basic
  Vanilla Sponge (page 11)
200 g desiccated coconut
4 plain, shop-bought mini
  Swiss rolls
1 quantity Buttercream
  (page 14)
red food colouring paste
edible silver balls
12 mini chocolate drops
2 white chocolate buttons
black writing icing
2 chocolate-coated wafers

1.2-litre and 275-ml
  pudding basins, greased
  and dusted with flour
12-hole mini cupcake tray,
  lined with 8 mini paper
  cupcake cases
cocktail sticks
piping bag, fitted with
  a star-shaped nozzle

SERVES 12

Preheat the oven to 180°C (350°F) Gas 4.

Make the Vanilla Sponge mixture and spoon into the prepared basins until they are two-thirds full. Use the remaining mixture to fill the cupcakes cases, allowing roughly 1½–2 teaspoons of mixture per cupcake. Bake all the cakes in the middle of the preheated oven until a skewer inserted into the middle of the cakes comes out clean – 10–15 minutes for the mini cupcakes, 30 minutes for the smaller basin and 40–45 minutes for the larger one. Leave the cakes to cool in the basins or tray for 10 minutes before turning out on to wire cooling racks to cool.

Put the desiccated coconut in a dry frying pan and toast until lightly golden, tossing frequently to stop it burning. Set aside to cool while you start on the cake.

Use a long, serrated knife to level the tops of the cakes if necessary. Put the larger one, flat side down, on a large plate.

Take the smaller cake and put it, cut side down, on a board. Trim a little off 2 sides to make a muzzle shape. Arrange the head on top of the body, flat side down, and slightly forwards. Secure with cocktail sticks.

Peel the paper case off the mini cupcake and attach the cupcake to the muzzle with cocktail sticks. Arrange the mini rolls, (2 upright in front and 2 flat at the back) to make the legs.

Reserve 3–4 tablespoons of the buttercream in a small bowl. Cover the dog with the remaining buttercream, spreading evenly with a palette knife. Scatter the toasted coconut over the buttercream and press lightly to stick.

Tint the reserved buttercream red with the red food colouring paste (page 17) and use to fill the piping bag. Pipe rosettes around the neck of the dog to make a collar and decorate with silver balls.

Use the mini chocolate drops for the claws and white chocolate buttons for the eyes. Pipe a nose and mouth on the head using black writing icing. Finally, push the chocolate-coated wafers into the top of the head for the ears.

This is the perfect cake for the novice baker as it only requires two round cake tins and no tricky assembly or icing. It probably appeals more to a younger child. You could also use brown or black food colouring to make a tabby or grey cat instead of the ginger cat here, or you can ice the cake with Chocolate Fudge Frosting (page 15).

marmalade cat

1 quantity Medium Basic
   Vanilla Sponge (page 11)
1 quantity Large Basic
   Vanilla Sponge (page 11)
1 quantity Buttercream
   (page 14)
orange food colouring
   paste
2 green fruit pastilles
   or similar
1 small liquorice sweet
1 long liquorice strip
black writing icing

*18-cm and 23-cm round
cake tins, greased and
base-lined with greased
baking parchment*

SERVES 12–14

Preheat the oven to 180°C (350°F) Gas 4.

Make the Vanilla Sponge mixtures (separately) and spoon the Medium quantity into the smaller tin and the Large quantity into the larger tin. Bake on the middle shelf of the preheated oven until a skewer inserted into the middle of the cakes comes out clean – about 30 minutes for the smaller tin and 35–40 minutes for the larger tin. Leave the cakes to cool in the tins for 10 minutes before turning out on to wire cooling racks.

Reserve 4–5 tablespoons of the buttercream in a small bowl. Tint the remaining buttercream orange with the orange food colouring paste (page 17).

Use a long, serrated knife to level the tops of the cakes and make them the same height.

Cut about one-third off the top of the larger cake in a leaf shape (refer to the diagrams on page 20). Fit the smaller cake into the space. Cut the leaf shape in half to make 2 triangles and position at the top of the smaller cake to make the ears.

Cover the cat with the orange buttercream, spreading evenly with a palette knife. Carefully spread the reserved plain buttercream to make a tummy shape and the insides of the ears.

Position the fruit pastilles on the cat's face for the eyes. Slice the liquorice sweet into thin slices to make the nose and position the liquorice strip as the tail and the mouth. Use the black writing icing to make the whiskers and the pupils in the eyes.

Look out for a suitable elephant picture that will work well as a template for this cake, or just use the picture here. Photocopy and enlarge the picture to the same size as the cake and cut out to use as a template. Make the cake the day before you plan to decorate it. Once completely cold, wrap in clingfilm and chill in the fridge overnight. This will make cutting out the shape easier. Garnish the serving plate with Indian sequins and jewels to complete the theme.

indian elephant

1 quantity Extra Large Basic
 Vanilla Sponge (page 11)
1 quantity Buttercream
 (page 14)
black food colouring paste
red food colouring paste
black writing icing
white writing icing
red writing icing
yellow writing icing
edible silver and coloured
 balls
coloured sweets

*33 x 23 x 6-cm cake tin,
 greased and base-lined
 with greased baking
 parchment*
*piping bag, fitted with
 a star-shaped nozzle*

SERVES 12

Preheat the oven to 180°C (350°F) Gas 4.

Make the Vanilla Sponge mixture and spoon into the prepared cake tin. Bake on the middle shelf of the preheated oven for 40 minutes, or until a skewer inserted into the middle of the cake comes out clean. Leave the cake to cool in the tin for 10 minutes before turning out on to a wire cooling rack. Turn the cake the right way up and leave to cool completely. If you have time, wrap the cold cake in clingfilm and refrigerate overnight before continuing.

When you are ready to assemble the cake, draw an elephant shape on a sheet of paper the same size as the cake, lay on top of the cake and using a small, sharp knife carefully cut around the paper template. Use the leftover bits of cake for a trifle, in lunchboxes or to snack on.

Reserve one-quarter of the buttercream and set aside. Tint the remaining buttercream grey with the black food colouring paste (page 17). Cover the elephant with the buttercream, spreading evenly with a palette knife.

Put 3–4 tablespoons of the reserved buttercream in a small bowl and tint red with the red food colouring paste. Fill the piping bag with the buttercream and use to pipe rosettes in the shape of a cap on the elephant's head.

Use the remaining plain buttercream to make a leaf-shaped saddle on the elephant's back. Use the different writing icings to pipe decorative lines over the legs, trunk and neck, and as tassels below the saddle. Use the white writing icing to fill in the tusk. Decorate the elephant with edible silver and coloured balls and use the sweets to trim the saddle.

transport

You could frost this cake using Chocolate Fudge Frosting from page 15 instead of the black buttercream if you like. Look out for Jolly Roger images to cut out and secure to wooden skewers for decoration.

pirate ship

1 quantity Extra Large Basic
  Vanilla Sponge (page 11)
1 quantity Buttercream
  (page 14)
black food colouring paste
2 latticed chocolate bars
  or similar
red writing icing
yellow writing icing
sugar-coated chocolate
  drops
chequered liquorice sweets
  or similar
25 g dark chocolate,
  roughly chopped

33 x 23 x 6-cm cake tin,
  greased and base-lined
  with greased baking
  parchment
Jolly Roger pictures
  in various sizes
3 or 4 wooden skewers
glue

SERVES 12–14

Preheat the oven to 180°C (350°F) Gas 4.

Make the Vanilla Sponge mixture and spoon into the prepared cake tin. Bake on the middle shelf of the preheated oven for 45 minutes, or until a skewer inserted into the middle of the cake comes out clean. Leave the cake to cool in the tin for 10 minutes before turning out on to a wire cooling rack. Turn the cake the right way up and leave to cool completely.

Use a long, serrated knife to level the top of the cake if necessary.

Refer to pages 18–19 for step-by-step instructions on cutting and assembling the cake. Sandwich the pieces together with a little buttercream.

Tint the remaining buttercream black with the black food colouring paste (page 17) and use to cover the whole cake, spreading evenly with a palette knife.

Measure the gap along the side of the ship and cut the latticed chocolate bars to fit. Press them into the cake slightly so that they stick to the buttercream, making railings.

Decorate the pirate ship with the red and yellow writing icing, as desired. Stick chocolate drops on to the prow of the ship. Cut the chequered liquorice sweets in slices and position as windows on the side.

To make the gangplank, melt the dark chocolate in a heatproof bowl set over a pan of barely simmering water (do not let the base of the bowl touch the water). Stir until melted and smooth. Spread into a rough rectangle shape on a piece of baking parchment, chill until set (20–30 minutes), then cut into a neat plank shape with a hot knife. Push gently into the side of the ship.

Stick Jolly Roger flags on either side of wooden skewers and push them into the ship.

I have made this a pink fifties-type car but if your child
has a favourite car from a story book, use an image from
it as a template and tint the buttercream accordingly.

fifties-style car

1 quantity Extra Large Basic
   Vanilla Sponge (page 11)
1 quantity Buttercream
   (page 14)
pink food colouring paste
red liquorice strip or similar
black writing icing
silver writing icing
2 white chocolate rainbow
   buttons or similar
edible silver balls
red writing icing
pink tube-shaped sweet

*33 x 23 x 6-cm cake tin,
   greased and base-lined
   with greased baking
   parchment*

SERVES 12

Preheat the oven to 180°C (350°F) Gas 4.

Make the Vanilla Sponge mixture and spoon into the prepared cake tin. Bake on the middle shelf of the preheated oven for 45 minutes, or until a skewer inserted into the middle of the cake comes out clean. Leave the cake to cool in the tin for 10 minutes before turning out on to a wire cooling rack. Turn the cake the right way up and leave to cool completely.

Level off the top of the cake with a sharp knife if necessary. Cut out a paper template in the shape of a car, lay on top of the cake and using a small, sharp knife carefully cut around the template. Use the trimmings for a trifle, in lunchboxes or to snack on.

Set aside 2–3 tablespoons of the buttercream in a small bowl. Tint the remaining buttercream pink with the pink food colouring paste (page 17) and use to cover the cake, spreading evenly with a palette knife.

Press the red liquorice strip across the car and trim off the excess with a sharp knife. Use the black and silver writing icing to draw the outlines of the doors, windows and wheels.

Spread the reserved buttercream into circles for the wheels, adding the rainbow drops and edible silver balls for hubcaps.

Use the red writing icing to outline the car and trim the liquorice strip. Add edible silver balls for door handles and headlights. Write the child's name on the car with writing icing. Stick the pink tube-shaped sweet in the back for the exhaust pipe.

You can decorate this balloon simply in one or two colours or be as imaginative as you like.

hot air balloon

1 quantity Extra Large Basic Vanilla Sponge (page 11)
1 quantity Buttercream (page 14)
brown food colouring paste
red food colouring paste
green food colouring paste
blue food colouring paste
yellow food colouring paste
purple food colouring paste
black writing icing
8 chocolate matchsticks, about 5 cm long

33 x 23 x 6-cm cake tin, greased and base-lined with greased baking parchment

SERVES 12

Preheat the oven to 180°C (350°F) Gas 4.

Make the Vanilla Sponge mixture and spoon into the prepared cake tin. Bake on the middle shelf of the preheated oven for 45 minutes, or until a skewer inserted into the middle of the cake comes out clean. Leave the cake to cool in the tin for 10 minutes before turning out on to a wire cooling rack. Turn the cake the right way up and leave to cool completely.

Put 3–4 tablespoons of the buttercream in a bowl and tint it brown with the brown food colouring paste (page 17). Divide the remaining buttercream between 5 bowls and tint each one a different colour.

Refer to the diagrams on page 21 and use to draw a similar balloon shape on a piece of

paper. Make it as large as will fit on the baked cake. Cut out the template and lay it on top of the cake, then cut around it with a sharp knife. You should have 2 good corners of the cake left – cut these off in equal triangles (see diagram) and stick together with a little buttercream to make a square basket shape. Position the balloon on a large plate and spread the coloured buttercreams in stripes over the balloon using a narrow knife. Pipe lines between the stripes with black writing icing. Cover the underside of the balloon with brown buttercream. Push the chocolate matchsticks into the underside of the balloon.

Position the basket below the balloon and cover with brown buttercream, making a weave effect with a fork. Push against the matchsticks carefully.

Choose this cake for your child's party and you can complete the theme by putting plastic farm animals around the tractor!

big green tractor

1 quantity Extra Large Basic
   Vanilla Sponge (page 11)
1 quantity Small Basic
   Vanilla Sponge (page 11)
1 quantity Buttercream
   (page 14)
green food colouring paste
4 tablespoons raspberry
   or apricot jam
black food colouring paste
4 round yellow fruit sweets
liquorice twist or similar
black writing icing
yellow writing icing
4 yellow sugar-coated
   chocolate drops
chocolate sprinkles

33 x 23 x 6-cm cake tin,
   greased and base-lined
   with greased baking
   parchment
6-hole muffin tray, lined with
   4 paper cases and 2 mini
   paper cupcake cases
piping bag, fitted with
   a star-shaped nozzle

SERVES 12–14

Preheat the oven to 180°C (350°F) Gas 4.

Make the Vanilla Sponge mixtures (separately) and spoon the Extra Large into the prepared cake tin and divide the Small between the paper cases. Bake on the middle shelf of the preheated oven until a skewer inserted into the middle of the cakes comes out clean – 45 minutes for the cake and 20–25 minutes for the cupcakes. Leave the cakes to cool in the tin or tray for 10 minutes before turning out on to a wire cooling rack. Turn the cakes the right way up and leave to cool completely.

Level off the top of the cake with a sharp knife if necessary. Refer to the diagrams on page 21. Using a long, serrated knife cut the cake in half to give 2 smaller rectangles roughly 33 x 11 cm. Lay the 2 pieces one on top of the other and cut a square from the end (through both pieces) measuring roughly 11 x 11 cm.

Reserve one-quarter of the buttercream in a small bowl. Tint the remainder green with the green food colouring paste (page 17).

Place one large rectangle cake on a serving plate and spread 2 tablespoons of the jam over the top. Top with the second large

rectangle. Sandwich the 2 small squares together with another tablespoon of jam and position at one end of the large cake, sticking in place with the last of the jam. Using a long, serrated knife trim the windscreen of the tractor so that it slopes slightly outwards.

Cover the whole cake with green buttercream, spreading smoothly with a palette knife.

Tint the reserved buttercream black with the black food colouring paste. Spread a little carefully over the sides and front of the tractor to make windows and a windscreen.

Peel the paper cases off the cupcakes. Cut the top of the cupcakes to make them level and position the mini cupcakes at the front and the regular at the back. Fill the piping bag with the remaining black buttercream and use to pipe lines over the wheels from the outside to the centre. Stick a yellow fruit sweet in the middle for a hubcap. Stick the liquorice twist in the bonnet as the exhaust pipe. Use the writing icings to decorate the tractor. Add the yellow chocolate drops as headlights.

Scatter the chocolate sprinkles around the tractor to look like mud.

It can be quite time-consuming making these little trains so unless you have time and patience it would be best to reserve these for a maximum of ten party guests. Make the cake the day before you want to assemble the trains and once cooled, store in the fridge wrapped in clingfilm overnight. This makes cutting, assembly and icing easier.

steam train set

1 quantity Large Basic
   Vanilla Sponge (page 11)
about 10 tablespoons
   raspberry or apricot jam
10 plain store-bought mini
   Swiss rolls
1 quantity Buttercream
   (page 14)
red food colouring paste
green food colouring paste
blue food colouring paste
black writing icing
sugar-coated chocolate
   drops
wheel-shaped and tube-
   shaped sweets

33 x 23 x 6-cm cake tin,
   greased and base-lined
   with greased baking
   parchment

MAKES 10

Preheat the oven to 180°C (350°F) Gas 4.

Make the Vanilla Sponge mixture and spoon into the prepared cake tin. Bake on the middle shelf of the preheated oven for 25–30 minutes, or until a skewer inserted into the middle of the cake comes out clean. Leave the cake to cool in the tin for 10 minutes before turning out on to a wire cooling rack. Turn the cake the right way up and leave to cool completely.

If necessary, use a long, sharp knife to level off the top of the cake and trim the sides to make them straight.

Put the cake on a board and cut it into strips across the short side (refer to the diagrams on page 21). Each strip should be 4 cm wide, so you should get 7 strips out of the cake. Then cut each strip into 3 rectangles. This will give you 21 rectangles each measuring 7 x 4 cm.

Place one of the rectangles on the work surface and spread a tablespoon of jam across the top and over one end. Stand another rectangle upright at the jam end and press together. Place a mini roll on the top of the rectangle on top of the jam to make the engine. Repeat with the other cake pieces to make 10 trains. You will have 1 rectangle left over to snack on!

Divide the buttercream between 3 bowls and tint each bowl a different colour with the food colouring pastes (page 17). Cover each train with buttercream, spreading evenly with a small palette knife. Use the writing icing to decorate the trains, draw in the windows and write the name of each child on the engine.

Stick chocolate drops and wheel-shaped sweets to the sides for the lights and wheels, and push the tube-shaped sweet on top of the engine for the chimney stack.

This cake can be baked the day before and iced on the day of the party. However, the ladder should be kept frozen and added just before serving so that it remains upright.

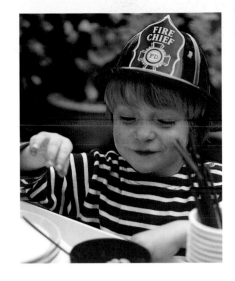

fire engine

1 quantity Extra Large Basic Vanilla Sponge (page 11)
1 quantity Buttercream (page 14)
red food colouring paste
3 tablespoons raspberry or apricot jam
4 liquorice wheels
round and square liquorice sweets
black writing icing
yellow writing icing
sugar-coated chocolate drops
blue food colouring paste
yellow food colouring paste
100 g ready-to-roll fondant icing or sugar paste
1 latticed chocolate bar or similar, frozen

33 x 23 x 6-cm cake tin, greased and base-lined with greased baking parchment
piping bag, fitted with a small, plain nozzle

SERVES 12–14

Preheat the oven to 180°C (350°F) Gas 4.

Make the Vanilla Sponge mixture and spoon into the prepared cake tin. Bake on the middle shelf of the preheated oven for 45 minutes, or until a skewer inserted into the middle of the cake comes out clean. Leave the cake to cool in the tin for 10 minutes before turning out on to a wire cooling rack. Turn the cake the right way up and leave to cool completely.

If necessary, use a long, sharp knife to level off the top of the cake and trim the sides to make them straight.

Using a long, serrated knife cut the cake in half to give 2 smaller rectangles roughly 33 x 11 cm (refer to the diagrams on page 20). Lay the 2 pieces one on top of the other and cut a rectangle from the end (through both pieces) measuring roughly 9 x 11 cm. You will only need one small rectangle so you can pop the second one in a lunchbox!

Reserve 2 tablespoons of the buttercream in a small bowl. Tint the remainder a vibrant red with the red food colouring paste (page 17).

Place one large rectangle cake on a serving plate and spread 2 tablespoons of the jam over the top. Top with the second large rectangle. Spread a tablespoon of jam over the small rectangle and position at one end of the large cake.

Cover the whole cake with red buttercream, spreading evenly with a palette knife. Position 2 liquorice wheels on either side of the cake and the other liquorice sweets as the ladder platform and flashing lights on top of the cab. Use the black and yellow writing icings to draw windows. Position the chocolate drops on the front as headlights.

Tint the reserved buttercream blue with the blue food colouring paste and use to fill the piping bag. Pipe lines around the wheels and across the front of the cab.

Lightly dust a clean work surface with icing sugar and knead the fondant icing until pliable. Add yellow food colouring paste and roll between your hands into a hose. Lay the hose at the back of the fire engine and coil around to the front. Push the frozen latticed chocolate bar into the top of the cake just before serving.

You can use Meringue Frosting (page 15) or Buttercream (page 14) for this rocket ship but as the Meringue Frosting is bright white, the finished result is more dramatic. Sparkler candles will make the rocket go off with a blast!

rocket ship

1 quantity Extra Large Basic Vanilla Sponge (page 11)
1 quantity Meringue Frosting (page 15) or Buttercream (page 14)
red writing icing
blue and red sugar-coated chocolate drops
edible silver balls
'flying saucer' sherbert sweets
rainbow puffed rice sweets

33 x 23 x 6-cm cake tin, greased and base-lined with greased baking parchment
silver candles

SERVES 12–14

Preheat the oven to 180°C (350°F) Gas 4.

Make the Vanilla Sponge mixture and spoon into the prepared cake tin. Bake on the middle shelf of the preheated oven for 45 minutes, or until a skewer inserted into the middle of the cake comes out clean. Leave the cake to cool in the tin for 10 minutes before turning out on to a wire cooling rack. Turn the cake the right way up and leave to cool completely.

Level off the top of the cake with a sharp knife if necessary. Place on a large serving plate.

Refer to the diagrams on page 21 and use to draw a similar rocket shape on a piece of paper. Make it as large as will fit on the baked cake. Cut out the template and lay it on top of the cake, then cut around it with a sharp knife. You should have 2 good corners of the cake left to use as jets – position these upside down on either side of the rocket, at the base.

Working quickly, spread the Meringue Frosting over the top and sides of the rocket, spreading evenly with palette knife. Use a little of the frosting to glue the jets into place.

Use the red writing icing to decorate the rocket and write the child's name up the side, if you like. Decorate with chocolate drops and silver balls. Set aside for 30 minutes for the meringue to harden slightly.

Push the candles into the base of the rocket. Scatter 'flying saucer' sweets and rainbow puffed rice around the cake as space debris.

Light the candles carefully and serve.

fantasy

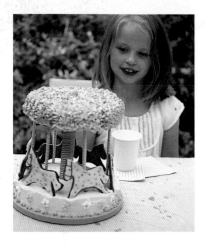

I have covered dowelling in pretty ribbons for the carousel but you could also use sticks of rock. To support the top of the carousel you will need the cardboard tube from a roll of clingfilm or similar, and a foil-covered cake board slightly smaller than 20 cm in diameter.

magical carousel

1 quantity Extra Large Basic
   Vanilla Sponge (page 11)
1 quantity Glacé Icing
   (page 15)
1 quantity Gingerbread
   Shapes (page 12) or
   Shortbread (page 13),
   baked into horse shapes
sparkly writing icing
black writing icing
1 quantity Buttercream
   (page 14)
pink food colouring paste
lilac food colouring paste
edible metallic balls
1 mini sugar-coated
   chocolate egg
sugar flowers

20-cm and 23-cm round
*   springform cake tins,*
*   greased and base-lined*
*   with greased baking*
*   parchment*
assorted ribbons
6 x 20-cm dowelling rods
20-cm cardboard tube
2 piping bags, fitted with
*   star-shaped nozzles*
foil-covered cake board

SERVES 12–14

Preheat the oven to 180°C (350°F) Gas 4.

Make the Vanilla Sponge mixture and divide between the prepared cake tins. Bake on the middle shelf of the preheated oven until a skewer inserted into the middle of the cakes comes out clean – 30–35 minutes for the smaller tin and 40 minutes for the larger one. Leave the cakes to cool in the tins for 10 minutes before turning out on to wire cooling racks.

Meanwhile, spread Glacé Icing over the horse shapes with the back of a spoon. Leave to set for at least 2 hours. Use sparkly writing icing to decorate the horses and the black writing icing to draw bridles and eyes on the horses' faces. Leave to dry for a further hour.

Wrap a ribbon around each dowelling rod and the cardboard tube and secure the ends with sticky tape.

When you are ready to assemble the carousel, put the larger cake on a serving plate. Use a long, serrated knife to level the top of the cake if necessary. Spread just less than half the buttercream over the top and sides of the cake, spreading evenly with a palette knife.

Divide the remaining buttercream between 2 bowls and tint them pink and blue with the food colouring pastes (page 17). Fill the piping bags with the buttercream.

Place the second cake on a foil-covered cake board that is slightly smaller than the cake. Pipe buttercream rosettes in coloured sections over the top and sides of the cake and scatter with assorted edible balls. Use more of the sparkly writing icing to pipe lines between the coloured sections. Finish with a mini sugar-coated egg in the centre.

Stick sugar flowers along the bottom cake and finish by piping little rosettes along the bottom and decorating with more edible metallic balls.

Push the ribbon-covered cardboard tube into the middle of the bottom cake all the way down to the plate. Arrange the dowelling around the edges of the cake at even intervals and push to the bottom of the cake. Rest one iced horse against each piece of dowelling.

Just before you are ready to serve the cake, very carefully place the top cake on top of the dowelling. Serve immediately.

The perfect cake for a party with a witches and wizards theme. Try to find magic candles that re-light to complete the spooky theme.

spooky spell book

1 quantity Extra Large
   Basic Chocolate Sponge
   (page 11)
1 quantity Medium Basic
   Vanilla Sponge (page 11)
1 quantity Chocolate Fudge
   Frosting (page 15)
½ quantity Buttercream
   (page 14)
black writing icing
silver writing icing
edible silver balls
orange sprinkles and
   edible glitter
assorted Halloween
   sprinkles

*33 x 23 x 6-cm cake tin,
   greased and base-lined
   with greased baking
   parchment*
*piping bag, fitted with
   a star-shaped nozzle*
*piping bag, fitted with
   a small, plain nozzle*

SERVES 20

Preheat the oven to 180°C (350°F) Gas 4.

Make the Chocolate Sponge mixture and spoon into the prepared cake tin. Bake on the middle shelf of the preheated oven for 45 minutes, or until a skewer inserted into the middle of the cake comes out clean. Leave the oven on. Leave the cake to cool in the tin for 10 minutes before turning out on to a wire cooling rack. Turn the cake the right way up and leave to cool completely.

Clean the cake tin, then grease and base-line it again. Spoon in the Vanilla Sponge mixture and bake on the middle shelf of the preheated oven for 30 minutes, or until a skewer inserted into the middle of the cake comes out clean. Leave the cake to cool in the tin for 10 minutes before turning out on to a wire cooling rack. Turn the cake the right way up and leave to cool completely.

Use a long, serrated knife to level the top of the chocolate cake if necessary. Cut it in half horizontally to make 2 pieces of even thickness. Lay one piece of cake on a serving board and spread with 4–5 tablespoons of the Chocolate Fudge Frosting. Top with the

vanilla cake, spread with 4–5 tablespoons of the buttercream and cover with the second layer of chocolate cake. Cover the top and one long side of the cake (the spine of the book) with chocolate frosting, spreading evenly with a palette knife.

Fill the piping bag (with the star-shaped nozzle) with the remaining buttercream and pipe 'pages' on the remaining 3 sides of the book, leaving a narrow border. If you don't have a piping bag, spread the buttercream with a palette knife and drag the tines of a fork through it to create the effect of pages.

Fill the second piping bag with the remaining chocolate frosting and pipe an edge all around the top and bottom of the book, filling in the border you left around the buttercream.

Using black writing icing, draw spiders and their webs on the cover of the book. Draw a wizard's hat and decorate with silver writing icing, edible silver balls and orange sprinkles.

Sprinkle orange glitter over the book and scatter Halloween sprinkles around the book on the serving board.

The cupcakes and chocolate-coated cones for these hats can be prepared in advance and assembled on the day of the party. Try to find a good selection of ghoulish sweets to fill the cones with.

wizards' hats

1 quantity Large Basic
   Chocolate Sponge
   (page 11)
300 g dark chocolate,
   roughly chopped
18–20 ice cream cones
edible silver balls
1 quantity Chocolate Fudge
   Frosting (page 15)
assorted sprinkles
assorted sweets

*2 x 12-hole muffin trays,
   lined with 18–20 silver
   or gold foil cases*

MAKES 18–20

Preheat the oven to 180°C (350°F) Gas 4.

Make the Basic Chocolate Sponge mixture and divide between the foil cases. Bake on the middle shelf of the preheated oven for 20–25 minutes, or until a skewer inserted into the middle of the cupcakes comes out clean. Leave to cool in the trays for 10 minutes, then transfer to a wire rack to cool completely.

Melt the dark chocolate in a heatproof bowl set over a pan of barely simmering water (do not let the base of the bowl touch the water). Stir until melted and smooth, then remove from the heat.

Hold an ice cream cone over the bowl of chocolate and pour the melted chocolate over with a spoon until the cone is evenly coated, allowing any excess chocolate to drip back into the bowl. Scatter with edible silver balls, then stand the hats upright on a tray and leave to set.

Cover the top of each cupcake with a swirl of Chocolate Fudge Frosting and scatter assorted sprinkles over the top. Fill the chocolate-coated ice cream cones with sweets and stick one on top of each cupcake.

For the best results make the cake parts of this recipe the day before the party. They can then be frosted in advance on the day and the final assembly completed about an hour before serving. Fill with sweet treats of your choice.

pirate's treasure chest

1 quantity Extra Large Basic
   Vanilla or Chocolate
   Sponge (page 11)
1 quantity Small Basic
   Vanilla or Chocolate
   Sponge (page 11)
1 quantity Chocolate Fudge
   Frosting (page 15)
sugar-coated chocolate
   drops
red liquorice strips
   or similar
gold- and silver-covered
   chocolate coins
assorted 'jewel' sweets

24 x 12-cm loaf tin, greased
   and base-lined with
   greased baking
   parchment
a piece of stiff cardboard,
   cut slightly smaller than
   the base of the loaf tin
cocktail sticks

SERVES 10–12

Preheat the oven to 180°C (350°F) Gas 4.

Make the Extra Large Sponge mixture and spoon into the prepared loaf tin. Bake on the middle shelf of the preheated oven for 1 hour, or until a skewer inserted into the middle of the cake comes out clean. Leave the oven on. Leave the cake to cool in the tin for 10 minutes before turning out on to a wire cooling rack. Turn the cake the right way up and leave to cool completely.

Clean the cake tin, then grease and base-line it again. Spoon in the Small Sponge mixture (this is for the lid of the treasure chest) and bake on the middle shelf of the preheated oven for 20–25 minutes, or until a skewer inserted into the middle of the cake comes out clean. Leave the cake to cool in the tin for 10 minutes before turning out on to a wire cooling rack. Turn the cake the right way up and leave to cool completely.

When you are ready to assemble the cake, place the larger cake in the middle of a large plate or board. Use a long, serrated knife to level the top of the cake if necessary. Spread two-thirds of the Chocolate Fudge Frosting over the whole cake using a palette knife, dragging the knife across the frosting to create a woodgrain effect.

Wrap the prepared cardboard in aluminium foil. Spread a little of the frosting over one side of the foil board and stick the cake 'lid' on top. Cover with the remaining frosting. Decorate both parts of the treasure chest with sugar-coated chocolate drops and red liquorice strips.

Position the lid at an angle to the treasure chest and secure with cocktail sticks. Fill the treasure chest with chocolate coins and 'jewel' sweets. The sweets also act as an extra support for the lid.

Let your inner-fairy go wild with the pink on this cake! If you don't fancy making a fairy you could always top the cake with a toy fairy or princess instead.

fairy cake

1 quantity Medium Basic
   Vanilla Sponge (page 11)
1 quantity Large Basic
   Vanilla Sponge (page 11)
1½ quantities Buttercream
   (page 14)
6 tablespoons raspberry jam
edible silver and white balls
assorted sprinkles
1 large white chocolate
   rainbow button or similar

FAIRY
150–200 g ready-to-roll
   sugar paste (Regal Ice)
pink food colouring paste
mauve food colouring paste
yellow food colouring paste
black writing icing
sparkly pink writing icing

*20-cm and 23-cm round
   springform cake tins,
   greased and base-lined
   with greased baking
   parchment*
cocktail sticks
*3 piping bags, fitted with
   star-shaped nozzles*

SERVES 16

To make the fairy for the top of the cake, lightly dust a clean work surface with icing sugar and knead the sugar paste until pliable. Divide into pieces for the body, head, arms, legs, wings, hair and magic wand. Tint the body part pink with food colouring paste (page 17). Tint a little extra sugar paste mauve, roll into stripes and press to the body. Roll out a pair of legs and arms, a stick for the wand and roll out a sphere for the head.

Tint a piece of sugar paste yellow and divide it in half. Use one piece to make a star for the magic wand and stick it to the white wand stick. Cut the second piece into tiny strips for the hair. Very lightly dab the top of the head with a drop of cold water and attach the hair. Use the black and pink writing icing to draw a face on the fairy and to decorate her dress and wings. Leave to dry on parchment paper for a couple of hours.

When you are ready to make the cake, preheat the oven to 180°C (350°F) Gas 4.

Make the Vanilla Sponge mixtures (separately) and spoon the Medium into the smaller cake tin and the Large into the larger tin. Bake on the middle shelf of the preheated oven until a skewer inserted into the middle of the cakes

comes out clean – 30–35 minutes for the smaller tin and 40 minutes for the larger. Leave the cakes to cool in the tins for 10 minutes before turning out on to wire cooling racks.

Meanwhile, use cocktail sticks to secure the fairy's body parts together. Remember to remove the cocktail sticks before letting children tuck into the fairy.

Divide the buttercream between 3 bowls and tint one pink, one mauve and leave the last one plain. Fill each piping bag with a different colour of buttercream.

Use a long, serrated knife to level the tops of the cakes if necessary. Cut each cake in half horizontally and sandwich back together with a couple of tablespoons of the raspberry jam. Sit the larger cake in the middle of a large plate and top with the remaining jam, then the smaller cake. Pipe buttercream rosettes over the tops and sides of both cakes in alternate colours. Scatter with edible balls and assorted sprinkles.

Sit the fairy on top of the large white chocolate rainbow drop in the middle of the cake just before serving.

The shortbread or gingerbread recipe will make more crowns than you need to decorate the cake but any extras can be served alongside so that each child has their own biscuit.

princess crown

1 quantity Extra Large Basic Vanilla Sponge (page 11)
1 quantity Glacé Icing (page 15)
1 quantity Gingerbread Shapes (page 12) or Shortbread (page 13), baked into crown shapes
assorted writing icing
edible silver balls
1 quantity Buttercream (page 14)
edible red glitter
1 white chocolate rainbow button or similar

2 x 20-cm round springform cake tins, greased and base-lined with greased baking parchment
ribbon (optional)

SERVES 10–12

Preheat the oven to 180°C (350°F) Gas 4.

Make the Vanilla Sponge mixture and divide between the prepared cake tins. Bake on the middle shelf of the preheated oven for 35–40 minutes, or until a skewer inserted into the middle of the cakes comes out clean. Leave the cakes to cool in the tins for 10 minutes before turning out on to wire cooling racks.

Meanwhile, carefully spread Glacé Icing over the crown shapes with the back of a spoon. Leave to set for at least 2 hours. Use writing icing to pipe multi-coloured dots over the crowns and to draw outlines. Stick silver balls to the icing. Leave to dry for a further hour.

When you are ready to assemble the cake, use a long, serrated knife to level the top of one of the cakes. Place it on a serving plate and spread 3 rounded tablespoons of the buttercream over the top. Put the second cake on top, rounded side up.

Cover the top and sides of the cake with the rest of the buttercream, spreading evenly with a palette knife.

Sprinkle the top of the cake with the red glitter. Stick a white chocolate rainbow button in the middle of the cake. Tie a ribbon, if using, around the bottom of the crown, then stick the crown biscuits around the outside of the cake.

For this castle you will need three cakes baked in the same square tin. Two of the layers form the base of the castle and the third layer is used for the turrets. Use either the Meringue Frosting (page 15) or Buttercream (page 14) to cover the castle. I have made this a fairy-tale castle but by swapping the white frosting for Chocolate Fudge Frosting (page 15) it could be turned into a fortress. Use chocolate bars to make a drawbridge and dark chocolate to cover the cones.

fairytale castle

3 quantities Large Basic
    Vanilla Sponge (page 11)
6–8 tablespoons raspberry
    jam
1½ quantities Meringue
    Frosting (page 15) or
    Buttercream (page 14)
edible silver and pink balls
diamond-shaped sweets
mini pink and white
    marshmallows
red liquorice strips
    or similar
150 g white chocolate,
    roughly chopped
5 ice cream cones
assorted sprinkles

20-cm square cake tin,
    greased and base-lined
    with greased baking
    parchment

SERVES 20

Preheat the oven to 180°C (350°F) Gas 4.

Make one quantity of the Large Sponge mixture and spoon into the prepared cake tin. Bake on the middle shelf of the preheated oven for about 35 minutes, or until a skewer inserted into the middle of the cake comes out clean. Leave the oven on. Leave the cake to cool in the tin for 10 minutes before turning out on to a wire cooling rack. Turn the cake the right way up and leave to cool completely. Clean the cake tin, then grease and base-line it again. Repeat the step above twice more with the remaining mixtures.

Use a long, serrated knife to level the tops of the cakes if necessary. Place one cake on the serving plate, spread with 2 tablespoons of the jam and top with the second cake.

Refer to the diagrams on page 21. From the third cake cut out 2 x 8-cm rounds (with an upturned glass if necessary) and 4 x 5-cm squares. Place a square on each corner of

the castle and secure with a touch of jam. Sandwich the round pieces together with a little jam and place in the middle of the castle.

Working quickly, cover the castle with Meringue Frosting or buttercream, spreading evenly with a palette knife. Decorate with the silver balls, diamond-shaped sweets and marshmallows. Cut the liquorice strips into a door shape and stick to the frosting.

Melt the white chocolate in a heatproof bowl set over a pan of barely simmering water (do not let the base of the bowl touch the water). Stir until melted and smooth, then remove from the heat. Hold an ice cream cone over the bowl of chocolate and pour the melted chocolate over with a spoon until the cone is evenly coated, allowing any excess chocolate to drip back into the bowl. Scatter with sprinkles, then stand the cones upright on a tray and leave to set. Place a cone at each corner of the castle and one in the middle.

You can ice both parts of the toadstool in advance and then assemble it just before serving.

pixie toadstool

1 quantity Extra Large Basic
　Vanilla Sponge (page 11)
1 quantity Buttercream
　(page 14)
red food colouring paste
white chocolate rainbow
　buttons or similar
red liquorice strips
　or similar
red writing icing
assorted sweets and
　sprinkles

*1.3-litre and 1-litre pudding
　basins or ovenproof glass
　bowls, greased and
　dusted with flour*
*15-cm thin foil-covered
　cardboard cake board*

SERVES 12

Preheat the oven to 180°C (350°F) Gas 4.

Make the Vanilla Sponge mixture and spoon into the prepared basins until they are two-thirds full. Bake just under the middle shelf of the preheated oven for about 45 minutes, or until a skewer inserted into the middle of the cakes comes out clean. Leave the cakes to cool in the basins for 10 minutes before turning out on to wire cooling racks to cool completely.

Use a long, serrated knife to level the bottoms of the cakes if necessary.

Divide the buttercream between 2 bowls and tint one bowl red with the food colouring paste (page 17) and leave the other plain.

Place the smaller cake, flat side down, on a serving plate and level the top a little to make a flat surface. Cover the entire cake with the plain buttercream, spreading evenly with a palette knife. This will be the toadstool stem.

Place the larger cake on the cake board and cover with the red buttercream, spreading evenly with a palette knife. Stick white chocolate rainbow buttons all over it.

Cut the red liquorice strip into a door shape, stick to the front of the toadstool stem and decorate the edges with red writing icing. Repeat for the windows.

Just before serving, carefully sit the toadstool cap on top of the stem and decorate around the plate with assorted sweets and sprinkles.

This cake seems complicated but it just requires patience. You need to make paper templates before you get started. The cake keeps for 3–4 days in a dry place. Make it the night before to let the icing set.

hansel & gretel house

700 g plain flour

1½ teaspoons bicarbonate of soda

a pinch of salt

4 teaspoons ground ginger

3 teaspoons ground cinnamon

275 g unsalted butter, diced

150 g caster sugar

125 g soft light brown sugar

225 g golden syrup

4 large egg yolks, beaten

2 quantities Glacé Icing (page 15)

chocolate rainbow buttons or similar

flaked chocolate bar

assorted sweets and sprinkles

TEMPLATES

roof: 23 x 15 cm

larger walls: 20 x 15 cm

side walls: 15-cm square topped with equilateral triangle 15 cm across and 10 cm high

piping bag, fitted with a star-shaped nozzle
solid baking trays

SERVES 10–12

Sift the flour, bicarbonate of soda, salt, ginger and cinnamon into a large bowl. Put the butter, sugars and golden syrup in a saucepan over low heat. Stir from time to time until the sugar has dissolved and the butter has melted. Remove from the heat, pour into a bowl and leave to cool for 10–15 minutes. Make a well in the dry ingredients and pour the cooled sugar mixture into it. Add the egg yolks and mix with a wooden spoon until the dough comes together smoothly. Divide into 2 even pieces, flatten into a disc, wrap in clingfilm and chill for 2 hours.

Preheat the oven to 180°C (350°F) Gas 4.

Divide one of the gingerbread discs into 3 equal pieces. Place one piece on a sheet of baking parchment. Lightly dust a rolling pin with flour and roll out the gingerbread into a rectangle about 4 mm thick. Using the roof template as a guide, cut out a rectangle. Write 'roof' on the parchment so that you can identify the piece later. Transfer to a baking tray and bake on the middle shelf of the preheated oven for 15 minutes, or until deep golden and starting to darken at the edges. Repeat with another piece of gingerbread, making one of the larger walls. Use the remaining piece to make one side wall. Repeat with the other gingerbread disc. You should now have 2 of everything.

As each section comes out of the oven lay the relevant template over the section and trim the edges with a long knife. Cut out the windows and doors (reserving the piece for the door). Leave to cool on the baking trays.

Fill the piping bag with the Glacé Icing. Cover any unused icing with clingfilm. Take the front section of the house and pipe a thin line of icing along the bottom edge. Stand this on a serving board and hold upright with a jam jar on either side. Pipe icing along the bottom and sides of one side wall and stick together with the front. Repeat with all the walls, holding them in place with more jars for at least 30 minutes until the icing has set firm.

Pipe thin lines of icing across each roof panel and stick chocolate rainbow buttons on to them to cover the roof. Leave to set for at least 15 minutes. To attach the roof, pipe a length of icing along the top edges of the house and put the roof in place. Hold together for a few minutes. Pipe another line of icing along the top of the roof and under the eaves to secure. Pipe icing along the edges of the roof, allowing it to drip gently into icicles. Use any remaining icing to decorate the doors and windows. Stick the door in place slightly ajar. Stick the flaked chocolate in for the chimney and decorate all over with sweets and sprinkles.

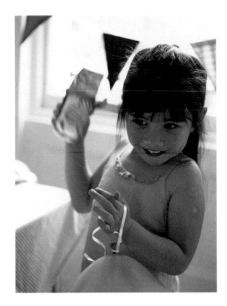

I have made this a three-layer cake but if you have two 20-cm tins you could easily make an Extra Large quantity of Basic Vanilla Sponge and divide the mixture between the tins. In this case, the cooking time for the cakes will be a little longer. This cake will keep in an airtight container in a cool room for up to 2 days.

box of secrets

3 quantities Medium Basic
   Vanilla Sponge (page 11)
4 rounded tablespoons
   raspberry or apricot jam
½ quantity Buttercream
   (page 14)
1 kg ready-to-roll sugar
   paste (Regal Ice) or
   fondant icing
pink food colouring paste
yellow food colouring paste
blue food colouring paste

*20-cm square cake tin,
   greased and base-lined
   with greased baking
   parchment*

SERVES 16

Preheat the oven to 180°C (350°F) Gas 4.

Make one quantity of the Medium Sponge mixture and spoon into the prepared cake tin. Bake on the middle shelf of the preheated oven for about 30–35 minutes, or until a skewer inserted into the middle of the cake comes out clean. Leave the oven on. Leave the cake to cool in the tin for 10 minutes before turning out on to a wire cooling rack. Turn the cake the right way up and leave to cool completely. Clean the cake tin, then grease and base-line it again with greased baking parchment. Repeat the step above twice more with the remaining mixtures.

Use a long, serrated knife to level the tops of the cakes if necessary. Place one cake on the serving plate, spread with 2 tablespoons of the jam and top with the second cake. Spread with the remaining jam and top with the final cake layer. If necessary, trim the sides of the cake to make them completely straight.

Cover the top and sides of the cake with the buttercream, spreading it evenly with a palette knife. Refrigerate for ½–1 hour.

Cut off one-third of the sugar paste, cover with clingfilm and set aside. Lightly dust a clean work surface with icing sugar and roll the remaining sugar paste into a square roughly 45 cm across. Loosely drape the sugar paste over a rolling pin and use to lift up over the cake. Using your hands, smooth the sugar paste over the top and sides of the cake. Trim off any excess from the bottom with a small knife.

Divide the reserved sugar paste and any trimmings into 3 parts and tint each part with a different food colouring paste (page 17). Dust the work surface with icing sugar again and roll out the coloured sugar paste. Cut into strips ranging in width from about 1–4 cm. Stick to the cake to resemble ribbons using either a little water, or some leftover buttercream. Set aside to dry for at least 3 hours before serving.

The cake, flower shapes and gingerbread people can all be prepared in advance for this cake. If you prefer, you could ice the cake in Buttercream (page 14) rather than Meringue Frosting (page 15).

merry maypole

1 quantity Large Basic
   Vanilla Sponge (page 11)
1 quantity Glacé Icing
   (page 15)
1 quantity Gingerbread
   Shapes (page 12), baked
   into small and large
   people
200 g sugar paste (Regal Ice)
   or ready-to-roll royal icing
assorted food colouring
   pastes
3 tablespoons raspberry jam
1 quantity Meringue Frosting
   (page 15)
1 stick of rock
1 regular marshmallow
1 mini marshmallow

2 x 20-cm round springform
   cake tins, greased and
   base-lined with greased
   baking parchment
piping bag, fitted with
   a fine writing nozzle
small shaped biscuit cutters
baking trays, lined with
   baking parchment
assorted ribbons

SERVES 10

Preheat the oven to 180°C (350°F) Gas 4.

Make the Vanilla Sponge mixture and divide between the prepared cake tins. Bake on the middle shelf of the preheated oven for 30 minutes, or until a skewer inserted into the middle of the cakes comes out clean. Leave the cakes to cool in the tins for 10 minutes before turning out on to wire cooling racks.

Meanwhile, fill the piping bag with Glacé Icing and use to decorate the gingerbread people. Leave to set for at least 2 hours. Reserve any leftover icing for later.

Divide the sugar paste into 4 parts and tint each part with a different food colouring paste (page 17). Dust a clean work surface with icing sugar and roll out the coloured sugar paste no thicker than 2 mm. Stamp out into different shapes with the biscuit cutters. Arrange in a single layer on the prepared baking trays and leave to dry overnight.

When you are ready to assemble the cake, use a long, serrated knife to level the tops of the cakes if necessary. Place one cake on a serving plate, spread with the jam and top with the second cake.

Working quickly, cover the cake with the Meringue Frosting, spreading evenly with a palette knife. Stick the royal icing shapes all over the sides of the cake.

Tint the remaining glacé icing with any of the leftover food colouring pastes and use to pipe dots around the shapes.

Secure the ribbons to one end of the stick of rock using sticky tape. Push the regular marshmallow, then the mini marshmallow over the top of the rock and push the other end into the middle of the cake. Arrange the gingerbread people around the edge of the cake, pushing them gently into the frosting to make them stand up. Serve immediately.

wildlife

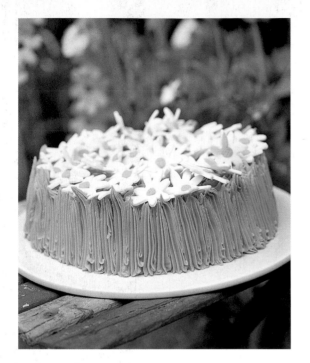

Make the daisies at least a day before you plan to serve this cake to allow them to dry and harden. They will keep for up to one week in an airtight container.

daisy patch

500 g sugar paste (Regal Ice)
yellow food colouring paste
1 quantity Large Basic Vanilla Sponge (page 11)
1 quantity Buttercream (page 14)
green food colouring paste

daisy-shaped biscuit cutter
baking trays, lined with baking parchment
cocktail stick
23-cm round springform cake tin, greased and base-lined with greased baking parchment
piping bag, fitted with a star-shaped nozzle

SERVES 10–12

Set aside 50 g of the sugar paste and cover with clingfilm until needed. Dust a clean work surface with icing sugar and roll out the remaining sugar paste no thicker than 2 mm. Stamp out into daisy shapes with the biscuit cutter. You will need 30–40 flowers and any trimmings can be re-rolled. Arrange in a single layer on the prepared baking trays. Rest some of the daisies against a wooden spoon so that they have a gentle curve.

Tint the reserved sugar paste yellow with the yellow food colouring paste (page 17) and roll into small balls for the insides of the daisies. Flatten each ball slightly and prick the surface with a cocktail stick. Very lightly brush the centre of each daisy with a drop of cold water and stick one yellow ball to the middle of each flower. Leave the finished daisies to dry for 24 hours.

When you are ready to assemble the cake, preheat the oven to 180°C (350°F) Gas 4.

Make the Vanilla Sponge mixture and spoon into the prepared cake tin. Bake on the middle shelf of the preheated oven for 35 minutes, or until a skewer inserted into the middle of the cake comes out clean. Leave the cake to cool in the tin for 10 minutes before turning out on to a wire cooling rack. Turn the cake the right way up and leave to cool completely.

Using a long, serrated knife, cut the cake in half horizontally to make 2 pieces of even thickness. Place the bottom layer on a serving plate and spread with 3–4 tablespoons of the buttercream. Top with the second layer. Tint the remaining buttercream bright green with the green food colouring paste and spoon into the piping bag. Cover the top of the cake with buttercream rosettes and pipe lines up the sides of the cake to resemble blades of grass, covering it completely and evenly. Stick the daisies all over the top.

Popular with younger children, this cake is a doddle to make – everything is done the day of the party and the decorating is very simple.

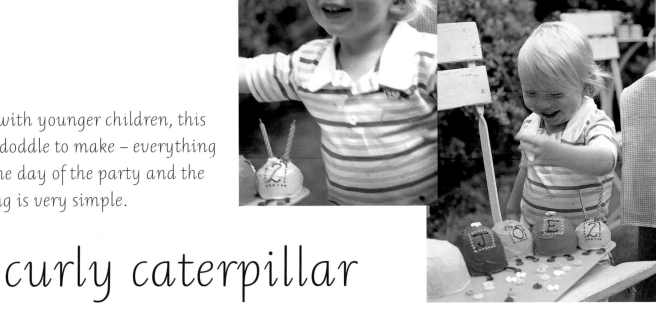

curly caterpillar

1 quantity Extra Large Basic Vanilla Sponge (page 11)
1 quantity Small Basic Vanilla Sponge (page 11)
1 quantity Buttercream (page 14)
yellow food colouring paste
red food colouring paste
green food colouring paste
mauve food colouring paste
blue food colouring paste
liquorice strips
16 jelly beans
2 sugar-coated chocolate drops
assorted writing icing

1-litre, 650-ml and 2 x 350-ml ovenproof glass bowls, greased and dusted with flour
6-hole muffin tray, lined with paper cases
2 green pipe cleaners

SERVES 10–12

Preheat the oven to 180°C (350°F) Gas 4.

Make the Vanilla Sponge mixtures (separately) and divide the Extra Large between the prepared bowls and the Small between the paper cases. Bake just under the middle shelf of the preheated oven until a skewer inserted into the middle of the cakes comes out clean – 45–55 minutes for the larger bowls, 30–35 minutes for the smaller bowls and 20–25 minutes for the cupcakes. Leave the cakes to cool in the bowls or tray for 10 minutes before turning out on to wire cooling racks to cool completely.

Use a long, serrated knife to level the bottoms of the cakes if necessary.

Divide the buttercream between 5 bowls and tint each one a different colour with the food colouring pastes (page 17). Bear in mind that the quantity of buttercream needed for each cake will differ depending on the cake sizes.

Cover each cake a with different colour of buttercream, spreading evenly with a palette knife.

Peel the paper case off one cupcake (and freeze the rest of the cupcakes). Cover the cupcake with buttercream. Arrange all the cakes on a serving board in a curly caterpillar shape and in decreasing size of cake.

Cut the liquorice strip into 17 x 5-cm lengths and position in pairs on either side of each cake as legs. Stick the last length of liquorice to the largest cake at the front of the caterpillar as a mouth. Position the jelly beans on the ends of the legs as feet. Stick the sugar-coated chocolate drops above the mouth for the eyes and stick the pipe cleaners in the top for the antennae.

Use the writing icing to spell out the child's name along one side of the caterpillar and to add more decoration, if desired.

Coloured pipe cleaners are readily available in craft shops and make great antennae for all manner of critters. If you don't want to make up a whole batch of cupcakes you could always use a store-bought cake for the ladybird's head.

lucy ladybird

1 quantity Large Basic
  Vanilla Sponge (page 11)
1 quantity Small Basic
  Vanilla Sponge (page 11)
1 quantity Buttercream
  (page 14)
red food colouring paste
black food colouring paste
1 long liquorice strip
giant chocolate buttons
2 yellow sugar-coated
  chocolate drops

*2-litre ovenproof glass
  bowl, greased and
  dusted with flour*
*6-hole muffin tray, lined
  with paper cases*
2 red pipe cleaners

SERVES 8–10

Preheat the oven to 180°C (350°F) Gas 4.

Make the Vanilla Sponge mixtures (separately) and spoon the Large into the prepared bowl and divide the Small between the paper cases. Bake just under the middle shelf of the preheated oven until a skewer inserted into the middle of the cakes comes out clean – 40–45 minutes for the cake and 20–25 minutes for the cupcakes. Leave the cakes to cool in the bowl or tray for 10 minutes before turning out on to wire cooling racks to cool completely.

Use a long, serrated knife to level the bottom of the cake if necessary.

Put three-quarters of the buttercream in a bowl and tint it red with the red food colouring paste (page 17).

Tint the remaining buttercream black.

Place the cake, flat side down, on a serving plate and cover with the red buttercream, spreading evenly with a palette knife. Stick the liquorice strip along the middle of the body and arrange the chocolate buttons on either side.

Peel the paper case off one cupcake (and freeze the rest of the cupcakes). Level off the domed top. Cover the cupcake with the black buttercream, spreading evenly with a palette knife, and place it upside down on the plate against the ladybird's body.

Stick the yellow sugar-coated chocolate drops on the head for the eyes and push the pipe cleaners on top as the antennae.

Look out for insect-shaped sweets or pretty foil-covered chocolate critters in sweet shops and gift shops. Complete the theme with some flowery cupcakes (page 122).

buzzing bee hive

2 quantities Large Basic
  Vanilla Sponge (page 11)
1 quantity Buttercream
  (page 14)
yellow food colouring paste
black writing icing
foil-covered chocolate bees

*23-cm and 18-cm round
  springform cake tins,
  greased and base-lined
  with greased baking
  parchment
6-hole muffin tray, lined
  with paper cases*

SERVES 12

Preheat the oven to 180°C (350°F) Gas 4.

Make the Vanilla Sponge mixtures (separately) and spoon one quantity into the larger prepared cake tin and divide the other quantity between the smaller tin and the paper cases. Bake on the middle shelf of the preheated oven until a skewer inserted into the middle of the cakes comes out clean – 40 minutes for the larger tin, 25 minutes for the smaller tin and 20–25 minutes for the cupcakes. Leave the cakes to cool in the tins for 10 minutes before turning out on to wire cooling racks. Turn the cakes the right way up and leave to cool completely.

Tint the buttercream pale yellow with the yellow food colouring paste (page 17).

Stack the cakes one on top of the other on a serving plate. Spread a little buttercream between the layers to help them stick.

Peel the paper case off one cupcake (freeze the rest or decorate them as on page 122 to serve with the cake). Position the cupcake, flat side down, on top of the cake. Stick in place with a little more of the buttercream.

Cover the bee hive with buttercream, spreading evenly with a palette knife. Use the black writing icing to pipe a geometric pattern over the bee hive. Arrange the chocolate bees around the cake and serve.

This is a perfect cake to get the kids involved in. They'll have great fun decorating their own flowers. The fairy cake recipe makes more than you will need for the garden but any extras can either be served alongside or frozen un-iced for use another time.

flowering garden

1 quantity Extra Large Basic
   Vanilla Sponge (page 11)
1 quantity Small Basic
   Vanilla Sponge (page 11)
1 quantity Buttercream
   (page 14)
purple, pink, yellow and
   green food colouring
   pastes
1 quantity Glacé Icing
   (page 15)
assorted sweets, sprinkles
   and chocolate insects
green writing icing

*33 x 23 x 6-cm cake tin,
   greased and base-lined
   with greased baking
   parchment*
*12-hole bun tray, lined with
   paper cases*
*piping bags, fitted with
   a variety of nozzles*

SERVES 12–14

Preheat the oven to 180°C (350°F) Gas 4.

Make the Vanilla Sponge mixtures (separately) and spoon the Extra Large quantity into the prepared cake tin and divide the Small quantity between the paper cases. Bake on the middle shelf of the preheated oven until a skewer inserted into the middle of the cakes comes out clean – 45 minutes for the cake and 20–25 minutes for the cupcakes. Leave the cakes to cool in the tin or tray for 10 minutes before turning out on to wire cooling racks. Turn the cakes the right way up and leave to cool completely.

Use a long, serrated knife to level the top of the cake if necessary. Put the cake on a serving plate and cover with two-thirds of the buttercream, spreading evenly with a palette knife.

Tint half the remaining buttercream with your choice of food colouring pastes (page 17) and use to cover the tops of the cupcakes (you will not need all the cupcakes and any leftovers freeze very well). Use piping bags with star-shaped nozzles to pipe flower patterns on the cupcakes.

Divide the Glacé Icing between 4 small bowls and tint each one a different colour with the food colouring pastes. Fill piping bags with small nozzles with the icing and use to decorate the flowers. Finish off with sweets and sprinkles. Position the cupcakes on the top two-thirds of the frosted cake and use the green writing icing to make flower stalks.

Tint the remaining buttercream bright green with green food colouring paste and use to pipe lines resembling blades of grass along the bottom of the cake.

Any leftover cake trimmings can either be used in a trifle or as a lunchbox treat. Feel free to go as wild as you like with the patterns on the butterfly wings.

bella butterfly

2 quantities Large Basic
   Vanilla Sponge (page 11)
1 quantity Buttercream
   (page 14)
brown food colouring paste
red food colouring paste
black writing icing
red writing icing
2 short liquorice strips
6 milk chocolate rainbow
   buttons or similar
assorted sweets and
   sprinkles

*33 x 23 x 6-cm cake tin,
   greased and base-lined
   with greased baking
   parchment
piping bag, fitted with
   a star-shaped nozzle*

SERVES 12–14

Preheat the oven to 180°C (350°F) Gas 4.

Make one quantity of the Large Sponge mixture and spoon into the prepared cake tin. Bake on the middle shelf of the preheated oven for 30 minutes, or until a skewer inserted into the middle of the cake comes out clean. Leave the oven on. Leave the cake to cool in the tin for 10 minutes before turning out on to a wire cooling rack. Turn the cake the right way up and leave to cool completely.

Clean the cake tin, then grease and base-line it again. Repeat the step above with the second quantity of Sponge mixture.

Use a long, serrated knife to level the tops of the cakes if necessary. Lay the cakes side by side on a large platter.

Draw one side of a butterfly onto a sheet of A4 paper and cut out to make a template.

Lay the paper template on one cake and, using a small, sharp knife, cut out the butterfly shape. Flip over the template and repeat with the other cake.

Set aside about 6 tablespoons of the buttercream in a small bowl. Tint the remaining buttercream brown with the brown food colouring paste (page 17) and use to cover the top and sides of the butterfly, spreading evenly with a palette knife. Tint the reserved buttercream red and use to fill the piping bag. Pipe rosettes along the outer edges of the butterfly wings.

Pipe the outline of a body in the middle of the butterfly with the black writing icing and outline the wings with red writing icing. Stick the liquorice strips into the top of the butterfly as antennae and decorate the wings with assorted sweets and sprinkles.

index

Author's acknowledgements

Huge thanks to Sandra Lane for her beautiful pictures and for finding good homes for the mountain of cakes at the end of each day's photography!

Thanks also to Liz Belton for her perfect plates, tableware and party pieces.

To Megan and Céline at Ryland Peters & Small for all of their hard work.

And to Mungo, for dragging me out of the kitchen and across the hills in all weathers.

And lastly, I can't thank my parents enough for their love, support and dog-sitting, above and beyond the call of duty. xx

Publisher's acknowledgements

The publisher would like to thank the wonderful models Aimee and Emma; Ava; Ashley; Bella, Bruno, Ella and Quincy; Elliott; Emma and Julian; Eva and Rosa; and Tabitha and Darci.

Thank you to Party Pieces for the loan of props. See www.partypieces.co.uk or telephone 01635 201844.